DAY TRADING

THE BIBLE

───── ❧❦❧❧ ─────

By Samuel Rees

This book includes:

DAY TRADING: *A Beginners Guide To Start Making Immediate Cash In Only One Day Of Trading*

DAY TRADING: *A Crash Course to Get Quickly Started and Make Immediate Cash in Only One Day of Trading*

DAY TRADING: *The Best Techniques To Multiply Your Cashflow In Only One Day Of Trading*

DAY TRADING: *Tips and Tricks to Start Right, Avoid Mistake and Win with Day Trading*

DAY TRADING: *The Advanced Guide that Will Make You the KING of Day Traders*

Additionally, the information in the following pages is intended only for informational purposes and should thus be thought of as universal. As befitting its nature, it is presented without assurance regarding its prolonged validity or interim quality. Trademarks that are mentioned are done without written consent and can in no way be considered an endorsement from the trademark holder.

TABLE OF CONTENTS

DAY TRADING:

A Beginners Guide To Start Making Immediate Cash In Only One Day Of Trading

By Samuel Rees

Introduction

Congratulations on purchasing *Day Trading: A Beginner Guide to Start Making Immediate Cash in Only One Day of Trading* and thank you for doing so. Day Trading is a fast way to make income on a daily basis, as long as you take time to learn the rules and do it correctly.

To help ensure that you get off to the best possible start, the following chapters will outline exactly what Day Trading is, and how it works before giving you tips and tricks to help you avoid the common pitfalls that beginners in the business often make. You will learn a step by step approach to buying and selling futures on the market in one day to make a profit. You will also see success stories of people who have been in day trading and are earning a consistent profit day after day. I am going to show you exactly what you can do to become one of those people!

Chapter 1:

What is Day Trading?

In this chapter, we will take a look at exactly what day trading is, and what you will need in your office to get started.

Day Trading Defined

Day Trading is also referred to as Short Trading. It is the buying and selling of securities within a single trading day. This can include futures, options, currencies, stocks and any other financial instrument. Securities are held rarely if ever overnight and only as late as the market closing on the same day.

Day Traders trade in any marketplace; however, trading is most common in the foreign market (forex) and stock market. A trade can last literally seconds or it can last the entire session. You might make only one trade per day, while another trader will make fifty or a hundred. Day traders don't look at the potential growth of a company down the road; they focus on what the immediate price actions of the securities within the company are doing that day.

How Day Traders Trade

Day traders employ many methods and techniques when making trading decisions. There are those that trade based solely on gut instinct to those that use elaborate computer systems to calculate the best probabilities. If you can master the skill of day trading, the opportunities for making profits will be endless.

One way that day trader's trade is to trade the news. It is a very popular technique. Scheduled announcements come in regarding anything from economic statistics to corporate earnings or interest rates, etc., and when the expected results are not met or exceeded, day traders act quickly upon the sudden large moves.

Another way day traders trade that is popular is called fading the gap at the open. That means that the opening price shows a gap, compared to the prior day's closing price. When you take a position the opposite direction of the gap it is then known as fading the gap. One day when there is no news, or no gaps, day traders will decide early in the day which direction the market is going.

Day Trading Markets

When most people think of trading the market, they automatically think of the stock market. However, there are several other markets to be considered when you begin your day trading career. In this section we will discuss those other options including the obvious stock market option.

Stock Market

If you want to day trade stocks here in the US, you will need to maintain a balance of at least $25,000 in your equity account at all times. What this means is that you must always have enough in your account to cover any loses that you might incur. If your balance would drop below that $25,000 then you can't day trade. It is recommended that you have at least $30,000 in starting capital to day trade the stock market.

Futures Markets

This is a popular day trading market. Futures are just what their name implies. They are agreements between buyers and sellers to buy or sell certain amounts of an asset at a future date. They actually take place in the future. Day traders make their money between the time that they buy or sell a contract and when they close the position before the close of the same day.

Selling futures takes much less capital then trading stocks. You need $3500 to $5000 to get started day trading S & P 500 Emini or ES contracts. These are one of the best futures for day trading.

When trading futures, the official market hours can vary depending on the contract that is being traded. So you should be careful to watch and make sure that you are out of your positions before the close of the day.

Choosing a Market

The market that you choose to day trade in will depend on several factors. Those factors can include your financial position, your trading system, your personality and even your interests. If you don't have $25,000, then you know that you aren't going to be day trading stocks. If you have a lot of capital, then stocks, futures, or forex are all great day trading markets. If there is one that interest you the most, then it would be a good idea to study it and learn all you can before you start trading it. Certain strategies seem to work better in certain markets also. Also the time of day can be a factor in your choice of your day trading market. No matter what you decide, a new day trader should never flip back and forth between the markets. It is stressful and it is not a good way to learn.

Chapter 2:

What You Will Need

There is a lot to learn about being a day trader. It may seem overwhelming at first. Don't worry, in this chapter, I will go over the basic items that you will need in your office or home office. I will also discuss some of the common terminology that you will run into.

In Your Office

If you are going to work as a day trader from a home office and do not already have one, the following will show you what you will need to both trade and be organized.

A computer with a good monitor: The majority of new computers these days have plenty of power to handle the day trading programs. Since you will want to have multiple windows open, it would be a wise idea to buy yourself a large flat-screen monitor as well. It will be much easier on your eyes.

A laptop or mobile backup: Since computers have a mind of their own and can shut down at any given moment, or have a software glitch, it's a really good idea to have a second copy of your brokers' app handy so you can switch over quickly should something happen.

High-speed Internet: You will need a fast reliable internet connection. Most internet companies offer business speed internet for your home at good prices.

Software: Microsoft Excel is spreadsheet software and will help you track your performance. It will also help you to analyze your returns. If you don't know how to use Excel, you can go online and check out Excel for Dummies, or look for a tutorial on you tube.

Online Brokerage Account: There are many brokerage firms that cater to the needs of high volume traders. They offer everything you need plus low commission to those who make a lot of trades.

Know the lingo

Just like most businesses day trading has its own unique language. Below are a few of the key terms that you will come across.

Fibonacci Series: This is a unique sum sequence of numbers. Each number is the sum of the two numbers before it. It goes on and on into infinity. Here is how it begins: 0, 1, 1, 2, 3, 5, 8. 13, 21, 34, etc. Many people believe that these numbers are a sign of good trading opportunities.

Kelly Criterion: Mathematically, it is possible to trade with success according to the Kelly criterion. It shows that the percentage of the account that you are trading is equal to the probability of the trade going up minus the probability of it going down. If your testing and it shows for example, that the strategy you have come up with works 60 percent of the time and fails 40 percent of the time, then you would want to trade 20 percent of your funds, .60-0.40

Pattern Day Trader: This is defined by regulations as someone who has at least $25,000 on their account, and who does four or more day trades within a five day period. Those trades must total more than six percent of the trader's total trades. This is important for the brokerage firm in calculating how they handle margin activity.

Wash-Sale Rule: This rule is a lovely little tax trap that catches many day traders off guard. It says that if you buy a security and then turn around and sells it for a loss; you cannot deduct that loss if you have bought that same security within thirty days either before or after the day of the loss. In the same day, a day trader might buy and sell the same security many times. You can get around the wash-sale rule, however it requires careful planning and excellent recordkeeping.

So now you have learned what your office needs, and some of the lingo. You are all ready to sit down and go to work. Next, let's talk about what you will actually do in this beautiful home office.

One of the first things that you will want to do is to set up your stock trading account with any day trading brokerage. Three of them to look at are Interactive Brokers (IB), Trade Station, and MB Trading. There are others of course, but these three have been around for a long time and are well known.

After you've decided on the day trading brokerage, you will have to look at the charting software and you should pay attention to the trade management screens. Are those screens comfortable for you to use? Now look at the real time data screen. Make sure that is also comfortable for you. Make sure that you are comfortable with knowing where all of the information is. Make sure that you can read it easily and that you won't have any problem looking at it on a day to day basis all day long. If you do have any issues, there are outside software companies that you can look at. For instance, there is Ninja Trader, Quote Tracker, and Ensign. You may find a more suitable day trading or charting package through one of them.

The best thing that you can possibly do for yourself at this point would be to learn your day trading software in and out. Day trading platforms have simulators. Use that simulator until you know it up and down. Be as familiar with it as you are with yourself. You don't want to be stressed out and not know a simple function of the program that could make your life easier. Also, it's the best way to get to know the whole process. You can place orders in the simulator. You should play with the simulator until you know the ins and outs of the entire program. It will save you valuable time later.

Chapter 3:

Strategies

T he thing to keep in mind is that the best strategy of a day trader is to find something that works and repeat it over and over again.

Once you have decided on that one strategy that works for you, placing and entry, setting a stop loss and taking a profit, then get on the simulator and practice! That's the way you will work out issues with your strategy. You can go over it as much as you want until you see continuous profit.

The goal is to be able to control your risk. You want to be able to control your trade risk and your daily risk.

- The amount you are willing to risk on each trade is referred to as your trade risk. That should ideally be equal to one percent or less of your capital on each trade. You can do that by selecting an entry point and then setting yourself a stop loss. The stop loss will get you out of the trade if the odds go too much against you. You should also learn how to calculate the position size for futures, stocks, and forex because knowing your position size will also help to keep your risk low.

- The amount that you lose in a day is your daily loss. It is smart to set a daily loss limit each day to avoid huge losses to yourself. If you have set your trade loss at one percent, you may want to set your daily risk at three percent. In that instance you would need to lose three or more trades with zero winners to lose three percent. And if you have practiced using your software and practiced using your strategy, that shouldn't happen often. You want to keep your daily loses small so that on winning days, they are easily recouped.

Trading only two or three hours per day is very common for day traders. However, there are some who do trade for the whole session from nine thirty am until four pm, usually for the US stock market. All day traders are consistent in the hours they trade. They trade at the same hours each day whether they are trading for three hours or the whole session. Here are some of the hours you will want to focus on yourself:

- If you are going to be trading stocks, the best time of day for trading is the first hour and second hour right after the open, and the last hour of the day before the close. So between 9:30am and 11:30am EST is the first two hour period you want to find good trades. The biggest price moves and biggest profits are to be had at this time of day. Between 3:00pm and 4:00pm EST is a good hour of the day also. There are pretty big moves then also, however, if you are going to only trade for two hours in a day, then trade in the morning. That's when the market is the most volatile.

- If you will be trading futures, the opening time is the better time to trade. That would be between 8:30 am and 11:00 am EST. Active futures see activity around the clock, so the best trading times are a little earlier then with stocks. Futures markets officially close at different times and the last hour of a contract can also offer sizable moves for you to get in on.

- If you decide to trade the forex market, they trade twenty four hours a day during the week. The EURUSD is the favorite of the day traders. It is the most volatile between 0600 and 1700 GMT. These are the hours when the day traders should trade this market. The biggest price moves are between 1200 and 1500 GMT. This is when both the US and London markets are open, trading the euro and US dollar.

The Strategies

We mentioned before that day traders find a strategy and then repeat it over and over again. That is what we will talk about now in more detail. These are the basic day trading strategies that are used. There are many others, but these are the most common.

Scalping: Probably the most common of the strategies is scalping. It is a basic get in there and get out of there type of mind frame toward trading. Day traders will get in on a good trade and then sell as soon as it starts to show profitability. It's relatively safe and that's why a lot of people like it. You don't watch it and then hope it stays strong.

Daily Pivots: A day trader using this strategy would look to buy their trade at its lowest price during the day and then try to sell it at its highest price of the day. These times are also referred to as low of the day (LOD) and high of the day (HOD).

Fading: This is known as a risky strategy. Day traders will short stocks once they start to gain rapidly. The theory being that the stocks are over purchased and the traders who purchased early will be looking to sell because the stock is gaining and they are making money. The other traders may be scalping. This strategy of fading can be profitable when used correctly, but keep in mind that the risk is higher.

Momentum: If you are a person who would be interested in riding trends, then this type of trading may be a perfect strategy for you. The day traders who enjoy this method watch the current news and are watching for the trends being supported by the highest volumes of trades. Then they jump on the wagon and ride the waves until they see signs of it turning around. Then of course they are watching the news releases and they just start all over again.

Stop Losses: The use of stop losses is crucial in day trading. The market is so prone to sharp price movements and you could potentially see substantial losses in a short amount of time if you aren't careful. There are two types of stop losses which we covered earlier. The physical stop loss order and the mental stop loss. During your whole day trading career, it is essential for you to keep these stop losses in the front of your mind.

These strategies that I have given you are not miracle strategies. Just because you master one, it won't make you rich. The main secret lies in consistency. Always be looking at your strategies and evaluating them. Tweak them to work for you by adding other parts of other strategies to them. Use them to find your comfort zone. Find what works for you. It has taken many of the most elite day traders' years to hone and perfect their unique strategies.

If you are to be a successful day trader, aside from reading this book, you must have patience. You may wait minutes to days for a profitable trade to come along. You must be able to make smart decisions. Knowing when to get in and out of a trade is vital. There could be a profitable situation staring you in the face and you have maybe minutes to react. And of course you must be able to maintain balance. How you react to winning and losing is so important. One day, you can be on cloud nine because the day went perfectly. The next day you could be down in the dumps and depressed because you may have taken a nasty loss. You must maintain balance there for your emotional wellbeing.

Chapter 4:

The Trade

In this chapter we are going to take a look at making the trade from the entry to the stop. We will also look at trailing stops and also at position sizing. We touched on that a bit earlier, but now we will go into more detail.

The Entry

Many people out there feel that the entry is the least important part of day trading that there is. And some people think that a random entry is good enough to gain a profit from. Although many people feel that way, you should always carefully consider it as a part of your day trading system. There are actually two important reasons why you need to consider the entry. The first reason is volatility and the second reason is risk.

The trading set up can be configured so that volatility is relatively low for two reasons:

- **Expansion:** You want to enter the trade right before a period of expansion, since high volatility usually follows on the heels of low volatility. The expansion is what takes us right into the profit zone!

- **Risk:** It usually feels like we can't control a thing during stock day trading. But the low volatility gives us the opportunity to control at least one thing. Yep! We can control how much we are going to risk on the trade! Since the point is to keep our risk at an absolute bare minimum, we use the areas with small range bars to put our stops under. If you aren't paying attention to your entry setups, the initial stop will be too far away from your entry and the risk you take on will be too high!

This is chart is an example of low volatility and the chart below is an example of low risk day trading which lead to expansion.

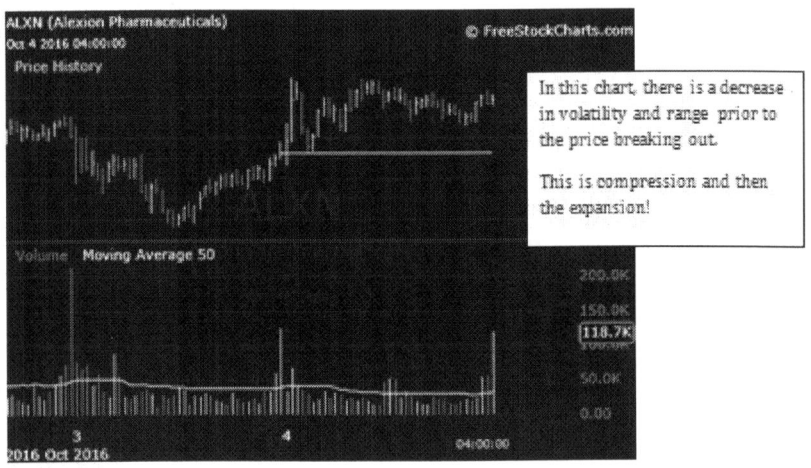

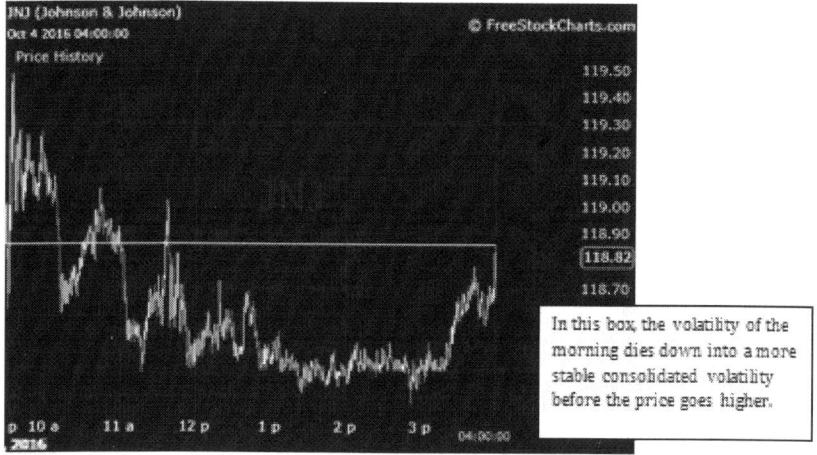

In this box, the volatility of the morning dies down into a more stable consolidated volatility before the price goes higher.

These two pictures represent triggers which much occur in order for the entry to take place. All of the day trading strategies will use this same kind of trigger.

The Stop

Yes. Here it is again. You will hear a lot about the stop, and here we will go into it in even more detail. I want to explain it a little further and once again reiterate its importance. It is definitely the one day trading rule that you can safely bet all of your money on. And it should always be the first concept that comes to your mind as you are experimenting and coming up with new systems or methods.

At some point as you begin talking to other day traders, you will hear someone say that they don't use stops period. Unless they are using some magic trading system that will put them back into a trade in a winning direction, then it's a crazy idea. Using the stop is your money's earliest line of defense. Since you are reading this and you are probably new to day trading, I will remind you again. **Always, always, decide where you are going to place your stops before you remotely decide to enter the trade!**

What the Stop does for you

Winning trades are fantastic and they tell you that what you are doing is right and is working. However, most likely the odds are that you will be using a day trading system that will bring you more losing trades then winning trades. But don't get upset! We all start somewhere! And how do we learn without mistakes? Right? At this moment you need to understand why you need to use stops and why they are so important because you are going to get stopped out of a ton of trades. And that's perfectly ok. It's normal to have many losing trades.

This is what's going to happen if you don't use a system with stops. You are going to end up calling your broker to ask him to send you a check for the small remaining balance on your account. Then you will go back to your desk, scratch your head, and try to come up with a trading system using those stops. So it would be wise to just include them the first time.

When you begin trading, you will decide for yourself what the amount of loss you are willing to accept will be per trade. It might be decided based on volatility, percentage movement, etc. No matter what method you use to determine your limit, the stop will act as your line in the sand. There is one big no for you to be aware of. Do not get into the habit of moving your stops out and away from the price as the time for it to stop you out grows closer. You will be screwed. It may not appear that way at first; you might see that it will help you on a few trades. But in the end you will be screwed so just don't get into the habit of doing it. Having wider stops may of course mean that you have a higher percentage of winning trades, but it also means that when you have a losing trade that it will be higher also.

The Exit

Earlier we talked all about how to cut your losses. In this section we will talk about letting your winners run. Technically the end of your trade is an exit. However, what we will cover here in this section will be about exits with profit.

Just as important as considering your stops, you should consider your exits. You want your day trading systems to have a positive expectancy. You need to make enough profit out of your trades or you will run the risk of a negative expectancy. We will cover expectancy in more depth later, but you need to know this information about it right now. If you have a negative expectancy you will basically be wasting both your time and your money!

You can never control whether your trade will be a winner or loser. However, just like a stop that you use to control what your loss will be, you use the exit to control what your profit will be. The exit strategy that you use has to allow your trade some wiggle room, but not get you out too soon.

The Exit Objective

You want to see your average profitable trade be higher than your average non profitable trade. You should set your profit objectives for more than the stop amount you have on your trade. In order to make a consistent profit, your day trading system has to allow for the winning trades to take off and run, so that you are averaging sufficiently more than you are averaging on your losing trades.

Profit Targets

This is a nice, simple and effective exit method that can be placed inside of your trading platform. It is placed at a dollar amount away from the entry price that you decided to enter in on. The great thing is that once you put this in place, you have nothing to do. You can completely leave your computer. You can go eat, or clean, or do whatever you need to do. Because no matter what, you can't control what happens with the prices after you set your profit target. And by walking away from the computer, it will keep you from messing around with your trade as you have set it up. It would be natural for you to mess around with your trade if you just sat there at the computer watching the prices go up or down. If you just walk away and let it go, what's the worst that can happen? The price will, hit your stop, hit your profit target, or be somewhere in the middle.

Position Sizing

Position sizing is really very simple, however it is the least understood trading concept. So in this section I'm going to try to explain it very clearly, because it is a very important concept for you to understand.

The whole idea behind position sizing is to prepare you for losing streaks and to get you through them. No matter how good your system is, you will have them. It's also referred to as trading money management. Position sizing has nothing to do with initial stops, or exits. Since, I've been mentioning stocks as my examples in these previous sections; I will say that position sizing is about trading how many stocks. That's the focus on the amount of stocks or futures or whatever, that you will trade.

Let's take a look at two different position sizing methods. The first one is the easiest. It's so easy in fact, a child can understand it. The second method is still fairly easy, but more detailed and actually it's the better way to manage your risk.

Equal Dollar Amount

One of the biggest mistakes that new day traders make is putting all of their eggs in one basket. For example: You are starting out with $50,000. You see a stock that you like and it breaks out so you put all of your $50,000 into that one stock. You place your stop and your exit correctly. You make money this time. And that's great! However, it's very dangerous and unlikely to keep happening. If you continue putting all of your eggs in one basket at some point you will lose. And it's not a matter of if. It's a matter of when.

So, here is the simple equal dollar amount method of money management. Instead of putting all of your eggs in one basket, if that was your $50,000, you would take it and split it. You could split it into ten equal chunks of $5000 each or into five equal chunks of $10,000 each. Then distribute your money among five or ten different stocks instead of piling it all into one. As a beginner I would suggest, splitting your money into five chunks to make things a little more manageable for you. As you learn more and have more experience, you can split your money into smaller chunks. And that's it! That was simple! Right?

Equal Risk Method

The Equal Risk Method is also referred to as the fixed percent method, and is a bit more detailed then the previous method we discussed. If you were to just split your money into equal chunks and then distribute it over five or ten stocks, the risk factor would be different for each stock. Like its name implies, the idea of the equal risk method, is to equalize the risk on all of your trades. What it does is determine the difference between the entry and the stop loss on each individual trade that you make.

The first thing you have to do is decide on a percentage that you are willing to lose on any one trade. Since you will have the percentage the same for every trade that you do, it means that the further out the stop on a trade, the less shares you can buy of that stock.

So, for example, if you are willing to lose ½% of the size of your account, then you are saying that you are willing to lose $250 max on any one trade. That is ½% of your $50,000. If you are going to only trade one stock that day and the stock is $.27 a share, and you are willing to lose $250, then you can buy 925 shares of that stock. Your stop is set at $53.47 x 925 shares so you are essentially using your whole account for this one trade. Below is an example of what it would look like on your screen. You will be able to see the entry point, the stop, and your risk.

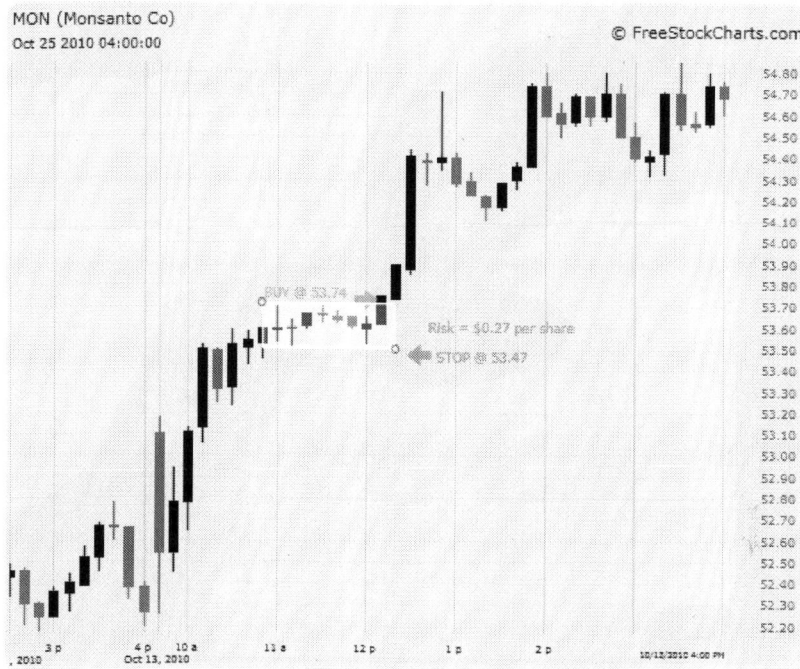

MON (Monsanto Co)
Oct 25 2010 04:00:00
© FreeStockCharts.com

BUY @ 53.74

Risk = $0.27 per share

STOP @ 53.47

If you have a small trading account, it is simpler to use the equal dollar method. As long as you are reasonable about where you are placing your stops, the risk is quite small on these individual trades. As your account grows and you begin doing more individual trades, then you will want to consider using the equal risk method also called the fixed percent method, because you are using a fixed percent decided by you for all of your individual trades.

Here is a word of advice if you are just starting out. Do not concentrate solely on your entries and exits. Stock market trading can be very nasty and unforgiving to those that do. You have to keep an eye out on your exposure while you are trading.

Expectancy

One of the biggest misconception in day trading is that you have to have winning trades all of the time to be successful in this business. Once you learn the day trading math this will make more sense to you. Expectancies formula will teach you that while the win percentage is important it is only a part of the stock market trading equation.

The equation

Don't worry if you hate math because this is pretty simple. And I'll show you some examples. The equation for expectancy is this:

(W%xAW)-(L%xAL)

W% = percent of winning trades

L% = percent of losing trades

AW = average of winning trades

AL = average of losing trades

In this first example I'm going to show you, I want you to understand that it is possible for you to make money with a low percent of winning trades. That's important. I don't want you to feel down if you have a low percent of winning trades. It doesn't mean that you aren't making money.

In our example we will figure that the day trader has many trades and only forty percent of them are winners. However, the amount of his winning trades' average three times more than his average losing trade so that means that his risk ratio is then 3:1. Three times more money in his winning trades then he's lost in one losing trade.

So the calculation would look something like this:

W% = 40% L% = 60% AW = $300 AL = $100

The expectancy = (.40x300) – (.60x100) = 60

This is a positive expectancy. A great thing, because now the day trader can expect that over the long term, his methods will yield a net profit. Even though his winning average is below 50% he is still turning over a decent profit. The key is to make sure that the amount of your winning trades is higher than the amount of your losing trades in order for this to work.

In this next example I will show you why having that amount of your losing trades higher are important. You can have many winning trades and few losing trades and still lose money. Expectancy works both ways.

Here, for example, a day trader is making trades and a lot of them are winning trades. Actually let's say 80% of them are. However, he continues to have some very big losses. Even though his loses are only 20% of his trades, they are five times higher than his winning trades are. That is not good at all.

So let's look at the expectancy calculation:

W% = 80% L% = 20   AW = $100 AL = $500

The expectancy = (.80x100) – (.20x500) = -$20

This is negative expectancy. You certainly don't need a high percentage of winners to produce profit in the market. That's only a part of the equation. In this example, the day trader had losses that were way above his winners. Eventually this day trader would have lost big if he had continued to trade this way. His system was definitely not working.

It boils down to the stock market being a numbers game. Everyone is looking for the perfect methods or systems to get them decent profit (numbers) while at the same time trading enough to use those numbers to their advantage.

I will leave you on this topic with this quote. I thought it to be perfect for the topic of Expectancy.

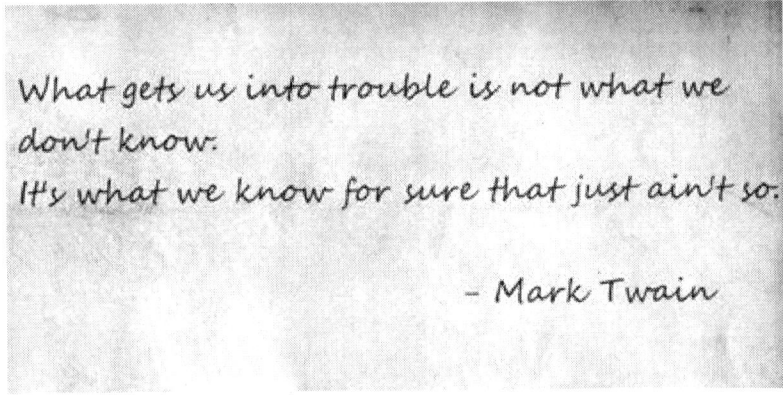

What gets us into trouble is not what we don't know. It's what we know for sure that just ain't so.

– Mark Twain

Price Action Trading

Different day traders will define price action trading in different ways depending on who you ask. When you are looking at the price charts, you can see all of the movement of the price of a market given over a period of time that you can choose. You can choose the current day, the previous week, the previous month, etc. The idea is for the day trader to look at the trends of the market for a particular stock and base their trading decision on those trends. Using lagging indicators on the price chart is just a big fat waste of time. The price movement will give you all of the signals that you need to develop a profitable trading system. These price movement signals are what are called the price action trading strategies. They give you a way to make some sense out of the market's price movements and help you to see what it's future movement will be with a great enough degree of accuracy to give you a high-probability trading strategy.

Below is an example of the nice clear chart that you want to be looking at when you are looking at price action.

Below is an example of a messy chart full of indicators. This is not the chart that you want to be looking at to determine price action.

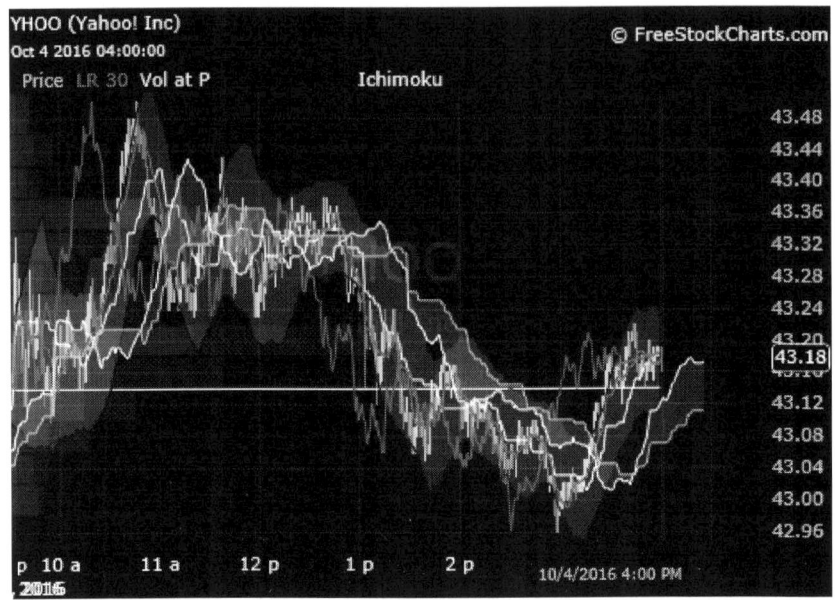

Fibonacci Trading

In this section we will cover day trading using Fibonacci levels also called Fib levels. If you are familiar with the Fibonacci sequence then this will probably be second nature to you. If you are not, don't worry, you soon will be. It's very easy to learn.

The Fibonacci sequence is a sequence of numbers where each number is the equivalent of the two numbers before it. It begins like this. 1, 2, 3, 5, 8, 13, 21, 34, 55.... Etc. After you keep going for a while, then you will take any number to the right and divide it by its neighbor and you will get .618. This is an important retracement level. It is also referred to as the "Golden Ratio". Then you will take any number on the sequence and divide it by the two numbers to its right and you get .382. This is another important retracement level.

The Fibonacci trading method can be used in two ways. You can either look for a stock with an already established uptrend using a 60 minute chart. Or you can try looking for a stock that is just breaking a trendline and starting up a new trend. When you are using the Fibonacci sequence in day trading always back it up with another system like price action patterns for example. Don't rely on them alone.

Forex Day Trading

The Forex market is one of the most popular markets for day traders. Forex trades are very basic and therefore are easy to understand. The trade is the same in that you have your entry and then you must place your stop. The big difference is that you are trading more than one currency.

Research

As in other markets, there is a lot of researching that you must do in the forex market. You will need to know which currencies are likely to rise in their value or fall in value over any time period. In other words you must decide which way two different currencies will move together when paired up.

One way that many successful Forex traders select their currency pairings is to correctly predict the outcome of data released in several countries which they do with their economic calendars. On a specific time and day of every week, all major countries announce how well one or more of their market sectors are performing within the country. That is where you will get the information that will help you to decide on which two currencies will move together best when paired up.

Expiration Time

Since you are day trading, you will need to pay attention to the expiration time of the forex trade that you wish to enter. All Forex trades have their own expiration time and you will have to make sure that you can close out by the end of the day that you enter the trade. These trades can last for minutes, seconds, or even the whole day, so also keep that in mind before entering into a trade. Know how long you want your trade to be active for. Many traders will decide on the longer expiry times, however, you can often make a very quick profit when placing a short trade that is one minute long. Especially right after a country has released their economic data.

Stop Loss and Winning

Just like other trades, know what your loss amount is going to be. Also know where your exit will be. You still must plan these trades and have a strategy just like in all other trades that you might be involved in as a day trader. One way to determine what your stop may be is to make it no more than 5% - 10% of what you want your winning goal to be. That way you are making a profit.

When you are new to the Forex market you will have to make a few decisions in regards to setting up your trades. Not only your strategies, but you will also need to have a broker.

There are a few different types of brokers to choose from. There are Multi Currency Forex Brokers, and there are Bonus Awarding Forex Brokers. You will need a broker so that you can fund your account in your own home currency. When you choose a multi-currency broker, you will not be forced to pay currency exchange rate fees when you make deposits into your account. Neither will you lose out through currency exchange rate fees and charges when making withdrawals. Bonus Awarding Brokers do just what their name implies. They will find you the best values and the highest value bonus offers as a first time trader.

Banking Options

There are plenty of banking options available to you. You can use a debit card linked to your checking account. If you don't want to do that or you are uncomfortable with it, you have the option of using a credit card, web wallet, or prepaid voucher. There will be many choices available to you. You may always open a demo trading account and test out the brokers trading platforms before you actually sign on.

Are Mobil Apps Worth Using?

The way that Forex Brokers have designed their mobile apps is in a way that no matter what kind of Forex trade you are trying to enter, you will always find them being offered to you through one of those apps. All of the same trades that you would place from your computer, and all of the same bonuses, offers and promotions are available to you on the Forex trading app. So I would recommend using the app. Especially as a backup of your trading platform. Computers are unpredictable at times. It is very wise to have a backup of your trading platform handy. Especially should something odd happen like a power outage right in the middle of a trade. You can just grab your phone and continue on with your deal.

Additional Fees and Charges

There are no additional fees associated with using the trading platforms to do your research and to enter your trades. The additional fees will come when you are signing up for banking options. They won't be fees charged by your broker. These fees will come from the third party businesses you use to make and receive payments. For example if you are using the web e-wallet or another service on the web. You will usually have to pay for third party services like those.

Ways to Limit Your Risk

Bonuses – When you first sign up to any Forex Broker as a new client, they will always offer you bonuses. You will be able to maximize your initial deposit and also take away some of your risk by using the bonuses offered to you.

Hedge your Trades – Another way to limit your risk is to Hedge your trades. This is a fine art and you should have experience and practice this well before putting it into use because you will find that you will be making multiple trades after you have entered your initial trade.

One way that some traders will hedge their trades is to claim bonuses at multiple brokers and then use the bonuses as the way to hedge the trades.

However, I must repeat myself. Hedging your trades is not something for a beginner to attempt. It is an art and has to be studied and learned before you can apply it. So you must be comfortable in what you are already doing before you can move on to this.

Trading in Syndicate – If you happen to know other day traders in the forex market, another way that you will be able to reduce risk is to form a syndicate with your friends, or your family. Maybe even your work colleagues if you are still working.

You do need to be aware that there are many terms and conditions applicable with trading in syndicate. There are terms about how many accounts can be in use at one time at any one address. Or how many accounts can be on the same computer. So if you decide that you do want to form a syndicate, then you need to really be aware of all of the terms and conditions.

Chapter 5:

Price Action Strategies

We talked about price action before. Now let's take a look at some of the strategies that you can employ using price action. Since it's one of the easiest methods, it's very suitable for beginners. Learning to manage your money is one of the most important things that you can do in day trading. Managing your money well is one of the ways you will guarantee yourself success.

Inside Bar Strategy

As its name suggests, this day trading signal begins with a gap up that will develop into an inside bar so that you then have a set up. If there aren't many stocks opening with a full gap, you may want to consider looking at a stock that is partially gapped up. This will be ok as long as they are above the previous day's close and below the previous day's high. So you have to look at these very carefully. Always do your research, but do it quickly.

So you have your inside bar. Now you want to place your stop. You want to place it right above the high of the inside bar. Now that you have your stop in place, it is a good time for you to decide where and how you want to exit the trade. If in the meantime your stop is hit, then just count it as a loss and move on.

Don't forget. Before you take that trade on, know where you are going to put that stop. Also try to have a clue about your exit.

Gap up or Gainer Lateral

A Gainers list is also knows as a percent change list. It is a list of stocks that is kept up to date in real time. They are in rank according to their percent of gain or their net dollar gain from the previous day. Stocks on these lists are in play. They will get a lot of attention from traders and will probably have a higher than usual volume.

On these lists you will be looking for stocks that have formed a lateral. When you find a stock with a lateral, that's when you will enter the trade and immediately place a buy stop above the lateral. Now what you are doing is waiting on a breakout to get a long position in the stock. Should the stock break out and you've bought it, and then make sure you place your stop immediately.

Now is when you need to think about your exit strategy. Know in advance if you are going to use a profit target or not on the trade and how you are going to set the target. This is always something that you should know before the trade is begun. It would be a good idea to plan these things in the morning before you begin trading depending on the trading you will be doing for the day. Make things easy on yourself at first. After a while, you will get a system in place and quick decisions will come naturally to you.

Gap Up or Gainer Triangle

As with the last strategy, the lateral strategy, you will be looking on the gainer's list or for stocks that have gaped up at the opening of the day. As you are looking at them, you will be looking for a triangle chart pattern. It can be at any angle, symmetrical or ascending.

Just like the previous strategy, when you see the pattern emerge, you can enter a buy stop order immediately above the triangle, or you can watch for the breakout and then place a stop right below the breakout bar or below the previous bar.

There are some days where it will feel like your stops are never touched and other days it will feel like the market is out to get you. Unfortunately that's just how it will go. But remember that it's part of the process and not to get discouraged or depressed.

Gap Up, Attempt to Fill or Breakout

This strategy is simple and is just as its name implies. It is a stock that has gaped up and is beginning to attempt to fill the gap. And it doesn't matter how much the gap gets filled. The only thing that will matter to you in this strategy is that the stock is attempting to fill.

The stock attempting to fill will require the price to go below the first 10 minute bar. It is also usually a sign that there is a decent supply of traders and they are currently short. They are anticipating the stock to go even lower. So when that stock does a 360 and moves back into the range of the first 10 minute bar, it makes some of those traders with short positions start to sweat. Why? Because those traders have lost whatever gains they had and are most likely now trying to figure out whether or not the stop they placed is going to be hit for a loss presuming that they placed it above the first 10 min bar.

Now what happens is the breakout comes in. It's usually fast paced and because of all the traders it will be on a higher than average volume. All of those traders that go short squeezed before are now stopped out so they are coming back in with a new long position which means that they are fueling the upside breakout even more!

Gap Up or Gainer the Afternoon Breakout

This is incredibly simple. Scan your morning lists in the afternoon. Repeat the same strategies from the morning. Usually in the morning there is a strong price rise. Then during the late morning and afternoon things usually calm down. And this is what you want to see.

In the afternoon version of these strategies, you will want to be looking for the stocks that are just kind of going nowhere. Then watch for one that seems to be inching its way up to resistance. That's when you want to place a buy stop order and watch close for a possible breakout. There are of course some stocks that won't ever breakout. But that's ok, because there are plenty more to try.

This trading strategy is like an old friend. It's easy to understand and comfortable to be around.

Fibonacci Retracement and Breakout

So far, this will be the most complicated trading strategy. Trading with this method won't even require you to use any indicators after you've become used to it.

Fibonacci Retracement Pattern

Prices move in a 1-2-3 pattern in all time frames no matter what you are trading. No matter if it's stocks, bonds, futures, etc. Every move made is followed by a retracement and then followed by another move up. You may not notice it right away because sometimes it is hidden within a bar on a chart. However, after you study enough charts, you will start learning to recognize it quickly.

We touched on Fibonacci day trading in the previous chapter so I'm not going to go back over the whole Fibonacci sequence and how you figure that out. The most important thing right now for you to remember is that Fibonacci day trading is centered on .618 which is also referred to as the golden ratio. You can find that ratio by carrying out the Fibonacci sequence far enough and then dividing any number by the number to the right of it. The two most popular Fibonacci retracement ratios are .382 (38%) and .681 (62%). No one knows if they are so important because they are naturally and universally fulfilled or because so many day traders know of them and use them continually creating a self-fulfilling prophecy.

Fibonacci Retracement Trading Strategy

Looking at a thirty minute chart, you will be watching for a stock that has made the highest high in the last two days. When doing this, you must have the 15 sma cross above the 35 sma on that day.

Then you will be looking to see the price give a retracement back to between 38% and 62% the next morning. If it is a bit over or under that's fine. It doesn't have to be perfect. Then what you want to see is the price to form a rising bar on the MACD histogram. The whole point is that you want to see a good retracement with some movement back in the direction of the impulsive move.

Once you have seen those things happen, you want to switch to your 10 min chart and watch for your breakout trigger.

Fibonacci Retracement Strategy Signals

The buy Setup: On the 30 minute chart the price makes lowest low in two days. The 15 sma crosses below the 35 sma on that day. The price has pulled back to the Fibonacci sequence level of 38%-62$ and the price also creates a falling bar on the MACD histogram.

Buy Trigger: On the ten minute chart the price breakout of a low of the thirty minute bar that creates the falling histogram bar

Exit: Price Target

Fibonacci sequence trades are harder to find because they aren't on a list and they don't just fall into your lap. However once you find them, they can turn into some very nice trades for you.

Gap Down then Gap Fill Inside Bar then Breakout

This strategy is a perfect example of a trading technique that takes advantage of other traders caught in a short squeeze who are on the wrong side of the gap.

A lot of day traders when beginning their career, will quickly grab a stock on the short side when they see it on a gap down list in hopes that it will keep falling for a nice profit.

It may appear backwards to go after stocks that have gapped down. However, some short squeeze action can bring them to life quickly and send them soaring like a rocket during the day. We talked about this before when people will reverse their position and then the stock will move up much more. If someone gets stopped out of a short position, they have to buy the same amount of shares that they shorted to break even. If they switch their position immediately, they are buying twice as many shares. That's how this intraday strategy can really boost a stock upward very quickly. If you can catch yourself on the right side of a few of these during the week, they will certainly make up for a bunch of small losing trades.

Inside Bar Strategy

The inside bar pattern occurs on a chart, on any time frame, when the bar's range is completely contained inside of the high-low range of the bar before it. Even just by looking this pattern is easy to locate on any chart during the day. If you don't feel like searching for it, there is always software that will do the search for you. The Inside Bar strategy uses multiple time frames to trade intraday from the inside bar pattern formed on a daily chart.

Reduced Volatility

When you see an inside bar on any price chart, it represents an immediate reduction in the amount of price action volatility. Often they will form after a time of price expansion and higher volatility. They can lead to formation of the laterals and the triangles that we talked about previously.

When you see these areas of reduced volatility they are a gift to alert traders. They are a representation of squeeze points and they offer important support and resistance levels that you can then use to your advantage. They are very important because these areas of squeezed or reduced volatility usually lead to areas of price expansion, and if you are a part of that you could potentially see significant profits!

Inside Bar Trading Overview

What you want to look for with this strategy is a bar on the inside that has formed on the stock's daily chart at the end of the day. When you find that, put that stock on your watch list for the next day. It is kind of like prepping for the next day or doing your homework. Then the next day you can watch that stock for a potential breakout of the inside bar's range on a 5 or 10 minute chart. Whichever you prefer is fine. The inside bars are also known as Narrow Range Bars and they perform better when using this strategy.

How to find Inside Bars

You can search for inside bars manually or you can search automatically by scanning the charts with the Average True Range Indicator. You will set the ATR to 1 day instead of 14 days which is the normal default. And that will allow you to find the stocks you will want to put on your watch list for the next day easily.

Please keep in mind that the day trading strategies we have gone over here are trade set-ups and not complete systems. They are meant to help you create opportunities to enter trades. You must refine them and add your own stops and exit strategies. Additionally, you will need to decide position sizing for each and every trade that you make.

Whenever you create a system, I would recommend that you test it. You want to make sure that it will have positive expectancy. You don't want to do the experimenting live on the market using your resources when you find out that your new system isn't up to par.

Also always keep in mind that future market behavior is not going to ever look exactly like the past. So when you are looking at assessment and quantification data this is something that you may want to remember. We just need to try to adapt it to the existing market as we go along.

Chapter 6:

Day Trading Tips

This chapter will include tips, rules and advice about day trading. They are not in any particular order, however, they are all important. It may be hard to see or understand their importance as you are just starting out, but over time and with experience, you will come to understand their importance.

A written Plan: If you are planning to trade without having a written trading plan, then you are going to find yourself all over the place. You will be wandering from strategy to strategy, from system to system and from market to market with no direction. You need to have a written trading plan to give yourself focus and accountability.

Trading simulator first: You will be saving yourself a lot of money by learning everything you can on your trading simulator before you do any live trading with real money. It is also a good idea use your simulator to test out new techniques before you apply them in the marketplace to make sure that they have positive expectancy.

Use an adequate account size: The minimum account size of a pattern day trader is $25,000. That's the absolute minimum. When you first start out, you will probably have some losses so you want to make sure that your balance will also cover that and also keep the balance above $25,000. If you are planning to trade stocks, the minimum account size is $50,000. Should your account be too small, you will have to consider other markets that don't require such a high balance. You can always move on to trading stocks later on after you start making money if that was your intention to begin with.

Stops: We've talked about stops a few times. Never ever trade without stops! If you are thinking that it would be ok to trade without them, then you aren't ready yet. And you should go on the simulator a bunch of times and see what happens when you don't use any stops. It will be a matter of time before you are facing a very big loss.

Setting initial Stops: Don't set your initial stops too wide. If you do, then you may not make enough profit to justify taking the risk on the trade. The risk to reward potential won't exist for a day trade.

Taking profits too soon: If you take your profits too soon you can actually lose money. I know it sounds crazy. However, most day traders are working with systems that just naturally may have less than 50% winners. And so that means that your winners must be at least a few times more than your initial stop so that you don't end up with a negative expectancy and lose money.

FOMC Fed Meeting Days: No trading. Just go have fun!

Do your Research: In order to maintain your confidence and keep investing your money in not just the market, but essentially in yourself, you need to do your research. It's very important to understand how the characteristics and statistics of strategies and systems before you use them or trade them. If you don't understand, you will completely bail out of the system or strategy the first time that you hit a losing streak or a drawdown. You must be familiar with the streak statistics of any system. You will have a much easier time of trading through a system's five consecutive losses if you have completely tested it and you understand that it's a common occurrence.

Following the Herd: A lot of new day traders will tend to blindly follow the herd. Unfortunately they then end up either paying too much for a hot stock, or may initiate short positions in securities that have already sank and may be on the verge of turning around. As you gain experience you will become better at making decisions in a crowded trade and less likely to stay in the trade for too long.

Market to Market: Starting out, it's not a good idea to move around from market to market. For example, don't move from stocks, to futures, to currency, etc. It can be a huge distraction and will prevent a new day trader from concentrating, learning all they can and excelling in one market.

Risk Management: If you want to be profitable, you must practice good money management. This falls in line with making a plan. A good trading strategy will allow you to have multiple loses without wiping out your trading account. However, the quickness with which those loses deplete will depend on what percentage you risk on each trade.

Treating it as a hobby: If you seriously want to make money at day trading, then you absolutely must treat is as a job and not a hobby. A hobby is collecting stamps or building models. You have to take the time to formulate a plan, learn, do your research, and decide what your goals are so that you can keep track of your progress.

Options Trading: Trading in options offers huge returns so for people who have a small amount of money to work with; this seems like a great idea. In fact, brokers actually require an additional application for this type of trading. On the other side of huge returns are huge losses. And someone has to be losing that money. It is a big mistake to get involved trading options until you have more experience. It is volatile and complicated and should be avoided until you have learned it well. If you listen to no other advice about where to begin trading, listen to this advice. Steer clear of options for now.

Leverage: We haven't really touched on leverage in this book, however, you are bound to see it mentioned. Leverage is equal to getting a second mortgage or using the title to your car as collateral. That's basically what it is. I don't believe it's wise to trade with leverage. And if you do your research and your homework and you formulate a good proven strategy that works well, you shouldn't even consider trading with leverage. Trading with borrowed money is extremely risky especially when trading such volatile stocks.

Risk – Reward Ratio: This is pretty simple. Try to keep your risk reward ratio at 3:1 so that you lose small and win big. Then your wins always make up for small losing streaks.

Chapter 7:

Success Stories

These are the stories of people who have made a success out of their businesses as day traders. Every path will be different, and by sharing them with you, I am hoping that you take something positive with you on your journey.

Mike

I began my trading career three years ago. In my first three months, all I saw was complete failure. I lost all of my money and was ready to quit, but I thought maybe I'd be missing the opportunity to have my own business. So I stopped what I was doing and began to watch, study, and practice.

I began watching the market and learning about the things that happened to change movement, reactions, and trading. I also began looking at analysis and learning how each analysis would predict and redirect the market and how I could use that to my benefit. I wanted to primarily trade forex, so I bought some books and studied them. I went online and created the free accounts and practiced my trading strategies.

After a whole year of studying, analyzing and practicing, I have developed my own strategy and I'm proud to say that it's working very well. Each month I am seeing a positive profit.

Mike

When I first started day trading, there were no computers with fast internet and pretty screens with all of the charts laid out in front of you. You had to go through the process of calling your broker and placing your trade and then waiting for confirmation of the whole trade from entry to exit. Eventually trade was allowed through touch tone phones. At that time, that was high tech. I thought about how great it would be to look at a screen one day and see everything right there in front of you. When I first started, my trades lasted a few days to a few weeks. There were no day traders back then for obvious reasons. I was using simple strategies that I came up with by reading books.

I actually did pretty well with my trades and I learned that I could make money. I would split my account up into parts and trade in multiple stocks instead of just trading in the same one.

When the computers came along and became more advanced and then the web was introduced, I took my knowledge and my day trading business was started. The cost of commissions came way down and it was great!

During that time I used long side breakout strategies and they paid off nicely. The market then was very forgiving. Everything changed in 2000 and the talk changed from lighthearted and fun to serious and all about protecting yourself while trading. Suddenly the stops became very important.

Since then I've traded a few different things such as index futures and ES and CL commodities. But I refined my trading skills before going on to that. The competition in commodities is fierce. Today I enjoy a successful career as a day trader. It allows me the freedom to do the things I've come to enjoy doing.

Conclusion

Thank you for taking the time to read *Day Trading: A beginner guide to start making immediate cash in only one day of trading.* I hope it was informative and able to provide you with all of the tools, tips and tricks that you need to achieve your goals both in the near future and for the months and years ahead. Please keep in mind that just because you have finished with this book, that doesn't mean that there isn't anything left to learn. Becoming an expert at something is a marathon, not a sprint. Slow and steady wins the race. Taking your time and doing your research will ultimately is the key to you building confidence and making money.

The next step is for you to stop reading and to go get to work applying the tools that you've learned in this book to become a day trader. Decide on what kind of trading you want to do and make your plan. Start building your own unique strategy. You never know what genius you can come up with. Have faith in yourself. Focus on trading one financial instrument to start. Trying to focus on too many different things in the beginning will hurt your chance of success and take away potential profit!

Finally, if you have found this book useful in any way, a review on Amazon is always appreciated!

Thank You!

DAY TRADING:

A Crash Course to Get Quickly Started and Make Immediate Cash in Only One Day of Trading

By Samuel Rees

Introduction

Congratulations on downloading *Day Trading: A Crash Course to Get Quickly Started and Make Immediate Cash in Only One Day of Trading* and thank you for doing so. In today's world, it can seem like nobody has any patience. We all want our phones to download information as quickly as possible, we want our friends and other types of people to respond to our emails immediately, and we want our Netflix movies and television shows to buffer as soon as we hit "go". It can seem like nothing ever stops. This is true in terms of finances too. These days, people want to make money even when they're not actively working. They want to see profits through the goods that they produce and through the decisions that they make for their money. It's safe to say that you probably feel similarly.

If you are looking for a way to make money quickly and with confidence knowing that you are making decisions that are backed by logic, then you've come to the right place. The following chapters will discuss how you can partake in day trading. Day trading, while it can sometimes cause exhilaratingly large amounts of anxiety, can also prove to be highly lucrative. The strategies that are presented in this book will help you to move one step closer towards making money in the amounts of which you've always dreamed. You'll be given tools to use that will show you what works and what does not work as you participate in day trading, you'll be able to compete with other people who are day trading globally.

DAY TRADING: A Crash Course to Get Quickly Started and Make Immediate Cash in Only One Day of Trading

The skills that are presented in this book are not simply learned overnight. They require commitment, and consistent research in order to be successful. Of course, your education has only just begun through the purchase of this book, but it's important to understand that you should never stop striving to be better in the world of day trading. There is always going to be someone who you feel is slightly ahead of your unique curve, and to keep up with the rather fast-paced nature of this industry, you're going to need as much help as you can get. Take time in the beginning to really set a good pace for yourself, and don't be afraid to finally take that next step and actually start day trading. Some people feel as if they're never going to be ready to actually purchase their first share, and they spend too much time learning. You have to know when it's time to act instead of plan, and this book will help you to do both.

There are plenty of books on this subject on the market, thanks again for choosing this one! Every effort was made to ensure it is full of as much useful information as possible, please enjoy!

Chapter 1:

The Basics of Day Trading Step-By-Step

Thee first thing to understand about day trading is that it is not the same as regular stock trading. It might sound funny to you, but many people who want to learn about day trading go into it thinking that stock trading and day trading are interchangeable terms for the same activity, because stock trading often takes place during the daily business hours of the work week. It's important to not confuse day trading wit stock trading. Here's why. Day trading can best be defined as when an investor purchases and sells a stock or share in the same day. None of the stocks that these types of traders possess are held overnight, and these people are often holding many stocks during a single period of time. While any type of market allows for this type of trading to take place, it is most commonly seen within the regular stock market and the foreign exchange market (also known as the forex market). If you are thinking that this requires a lot of fast moving energy and smart people in order for this to occur, you're certainly right. Day trading is mostly done by people who are not only well-educated, but also well-funded. Let's take a look at some key terms that you should be aware of before we get into a discussion of the steps that you need to take in order to start day trading as fast as possible.

Not a "Get-Rich-Quick" Scam

Perhaps one of the most important things to realize about day trading is that you should not be pursuing this or focusing on this avenue of wealth as a "get-rich-quick" scam. Be advised that there are countless scam websites that will lead you to believe that if you day trade using their brokers, your yields are bound to be higher than if you were to use another site. In general, make sure that you are vetting all sources that you use for day trading, and be weary of sites that ask you for financial information before providing you with any preliminary information in return. Additionally, another reason why it's highly debated as to whether or not day trading is actually a successful form of trading is because there are no well-known investors who have left the day trading market with millions of dollars that they previously had not had. For example, one of the biggest names in the stock market trading industry is certainly Warren Buffett. A name like this does not exist for day trading, and for some people this is enough for them to conclude that day trading cannot offer long-term, large profit margins. For the people who engage in day trading anyway, they claim that the high-risk and often confusing nature of day trading is primarily why outsiders don't think that there's much success in it. This is ultimately for you to decide.

That's not to say that day trading isn't hasn't been profitable for many people. If it wasn't, we wouldn't even be discussing it. The above paragraph was not meant to deter you from thinking about day trading; rather, it was to try to convey that you must be careful prior to taking action with your money in this way. The rest of this chapter will give you a step-by-step account of what you need to do in order to not just partake in day trading, but to partake in day trading well. After we've discussed the kind of capital that you need for this type of work and the other steps that are involved, we'll then move onto the skills that you should be cultivating, and the other types of traits that you will need to start thinking about obtaining.

Step 1 to Becoming a Successful Day Trader: Do You Have Enough Money

Even before you assess the personality traits that you possess to make sure that they coincide with the demanding nature of day trading (hint: this might be step 2!), the first step is to figure out if you have enough money to fund your venture. Typically, it's generally advised that you save at least $100,000 before you make even your first deal day trading. Before you freak out at the sheer size of this colossal number, it's important to understand that this amount of money is recommended for day traders who are looking to quit their day jobs and take day trading as seriously as possible. Of course, if you are not going to be day trading full time, this number can be small in scope; however, there are still some factors that you need to keep in mind. For example, especially if you are new to day trading there are bound to be times when you are losing trades ones after the other. It could be awhile until you finally make a deal where you win some money. Times can be tough for a day trader, and you need to make sure that you're financially prepared for when tough times strike. If you are thinking of starting out with less than $100,000, you should also be limiting how often you are day trading, which might be perfect for someone who is just starting out and is trying to get a feel for the environment.

Step 2 to Becoming a Successful Day Trader: Be Honest with Yourself Regarding your Capabilities and Limitations

Before you consider day trading, you will need to assess your own limitations and skills. Of course, this book will help you to develop the skills that you need in order to day trade, but the fact of the matter is that in addition to possessing knowledge about day trading, you will also need knowledge on stock trading in general. It's not enough to simply know about the process of day trading itself. I myself have written two books on the topic of stock trading, but there are plenty of others that exist on this particular subject. Other questions that you should be asking yourself include whether or not you're good at math, whether you're willing to make a commitment to the type of lifestyle that day trading often demands, and whether or not you have an awareness of how behavior plays a role in decision-making. Be honest with yourself as you contemplate your tendencies, and reflect on how you can include these types of traits into your lifestyle if they are something that you are currently lacking. As a day trader, you will be expected to take on a significant amount of risk, be able to teach yourself as you go, and work extremely long and sometimes rigorous hours. If these types of qualities don't seem all that appealing to you, it might be time to rethink this industry.

Step 3 to Becoming a Successful Day Trader: Have a Comprehensive Understanding of your Marketplace

Again, it's not enough to simply understand how day trading works by itself. As a day trader, you will still be interacting with everyone on the market, not just other day traders. Additionally, it's extra important to set a list of parameters and

64

guidelines for yourself so that you can work within them as quickly as possible. Between fifty to seventy-five percent of day trading shares are traded within a matter of seconds. If you don't have guidelines that you know like the back of your hand, you're more likely to make mistakes. We will talk about day trading strategies extensively in a subsequent chapter. Within the New York Stock Exchange, there are several important factors that you should be considering as you day trade. Let's take a look at some of these factors:

When to Purchase: One of the biggest struggles that a day trader has to deal with is to decide when to purchase shares of a stock in which they're interested. Unlike the regular stock market where you can wait to buy a stock when it's at a low price in the hopes that it will increase in value over a long period of time, time is not on your side when you day trade. Instead of looking at the stock market from a long-term perspective, you have to be able to pick out stocks that you think will do well in just a day. Often, a day trader will spend his or her time waiting for the "right time" to purchase a stock, only to end up missing it completely. If you see that a stock is at a low price, don't waste your time making sure that it's bound to rise in price extremely quickly. Instead, purchase the stock and make a small profit throughout the day while you can. If you're already used to trading on the regular stock market, thinking about the market in this way can seem like a big shift. Instead of thinking long-term, day traders think in the short term so that they can maximize their profits as quickly as possible.

When to sell: In conjunction with figuring out when you should be buying a particular stock so that you can sell it later in the day, another market factor that a day trader must figure out is at what point he or she should be selling their particular stock. One of the biggest mistakes that a preliminary day trader can make is to become complacent with the potential of one of the stocks that they hold. For example, if you are used to a stock of Geico increasing in value over the course of a day, you should work against the notion in your head that this trend will continue forever. Becoming used to patterns is one of the reasons why day trading can be so exciting and frustrating at the same time. If you have reason to believe that a particular stock is going to take a turn for the negative in the near future, get out while you're still making a profit. Additionally, if you find yourself in a position where you have lost money because you sold when it was too late, don't get down on yourself. More importantly, don't let this loss influence how well you negotiate your next trade. The emotional as well as the logical are both important aspects of day trading.

Start Small: You will need to develop your trading processes slowly over time. Even if you've been trading in the stock market for a significant period of time, you will have to get used to the nuances that exist within day trading. Instead of learning the basics of day trading and jumping right into making your own trades, you should consider first practicing on a fake market. One of the best tools that currently exist on the internet for this type of practice is known as the Stock Simulator by Investopedia. This device can help you to feel more confident in trading quickly and holding many stocks at the same time. Of course, this type of tool might not be as exciting as the real thing, but if you want a safe environment where you can't lose money over silly mistakes, this is the place to go.

Qualities that You Must Cultivate in Order to Day Trade Well

There are a number of characteristics that you're going to have to cultivate in order to day trade well. While there are certainly people who avoid day trading like the plague, there are just as many and more who are treating day trading like the great opportunity that it is.

Chapter 2:

Brokerage Firms that Focus on Day Trading

Hopefully the first chapter was able to provide you with an easy transition into what day trading is all about. Of course, we are only getting started. Now that you know the sort of capital that you need and the types of preliminary factors with which to be concerned, it's time to get more technical. If you've already learned about stock trading in general, it's likely that you already know a thing or two about brokers.

As a refresher, a broker or a brokerage firm is a company that serves as the middleman between the individual investor (you) and the stock market at large. The reason why brokers are necessary is because in order to make trades on the stock market, you need to obtain a license. All brokers have these licenses. In exchange for "use" of these licenses, a broker will charge you a commission fee on all the transactions that you make. While there are differences between the types of accounts that you can open with a broker, this definition is basically all that a broker does. This chapter will focus on how a broker with a focus on day trading will differ from a broker with a focus on the regular stock market. As an aspiring day

trader, you're going to want to make sure that you hire a
broker with a focus on your specific field.

Day Trading Commission Rates

The first thing that is important to note about commission
rates in general is that there is not really an "average rate" that
you can expect to pay. Broker services vary depending on the
level of service that they are going to provide you as well as the
complexity of the type of stock that's being traded. For
example, a discounted brokerage service might only charge ten
dollars, but they may also only deal with certain types of stock.
At the opposite end of the spectrum, a more advanced
brokerage firm might charge you one hundred dollars, but
they may also promise to offer you advice and keep an eye on
the overall health of your portfolio. The best piece of advice
here is to work within your own budget and work to find a
broker that offers the amount of services that you're expecting.
Most importantly, whichever rate you choose, the profit that
you're seeing should be covering the cost of your brokerage
fees. If this isn't happening, you need to reevaluate your
commission strategy.

As you begin to look for a broker, another aspect that pertains
to day trading in particular is that you sometimes can make a
deal with them because of the fact that you're going to be
trading so often. For example, if a firm's rate is typically $50,
you might be able to talk them down to $40 if you agree to
make at least fifty trades per month. Depending on the
broker, this could be a great deal for you. Another type of
break that some brokers allow for day traders is one where the
investor can pay annually instead of monthly. This type of
commission is known as a fixed annual percentage fee. If you
can negotiate this with a broker, you'll have a concrete figure

that you'll have to break even with for the entire year. This can help you to set goals for yourself based on the money that you'll have to pay back at the end of the year. This way, you'll have a better gauge from which you can operate.

One other important factor that you need to recognize before we move onto looking at the best day trading brokers out there is that brokers can go broke if the market conditions change quickly. For example, in 2015 a company by the name of Alpari UK had to shut its doors after the Swiss National Bank decided to equal the playing field between the franc and the euro. Some brokerage firms that had sufficient capital were able to survive this shift, but Alpari UK was not one of them. When a brokerage company goes bankrupt, you lose your money. To avoid these types of situations, it's important that you find reputable stock brokers who have a reputation for having sufficient capital on hand.

Let's take a look at some of the best day trading companies that exist for day traders. Most of the companies are not only reputable, they also have the capital backing them to prove it. Many day traders today have turned to the internet to provide them with the best forums for trading online. The reason for this is primarily because trading can happen faster than it can through transactions that are made between the individual investor and a physical broker in person. For these reasons, many of the best brokers available to day traders today can be found online. Let's take a look at some of the best brokers that exist on the market today for day traders.

1. **Interactive Brokers:** Interactive brokers is a company that offers a wide variety of services to the investor who is interested in day trading. As of 2015, Interactive Brokers was considered the best online trading forum for day traders. The commission rates

can best be defined as fair to the individual investor,
and there is no trading fee to start using their services.
Per share, the company will take just .005 cents from
you. That's pretty hard to beat. In addition to being
known as interactive brokers, the company is also
sometimes referred to as simply IB.

1. **2.thinkorswim:** thinkorswim is owned by TD Bank
   Ameritrade. This online brokerage firm can offer you
   not only a brokerage service, but also interactive studies
   and charts that are unique to the individual stocks in
   which you're choosing to invest. Of course, throughout
   the day you may not have time to look at charts that
   compare one stock to another, because of the fact that
   you're going to be trying to trade shares as-quickly-as
   possible, but this type of data-driven advice can help
   you to make choices for your stocks in the future. Other
   resources that this firm can provide include software,
   advice chatrooms and a forum where someone from TD
   actually broadcasts what's going on the stock exchange
   floor. For an investor who is looking for advice as well
   as a brokerage service, this might be perfect. One factor
   that can be a deterrent for TD Bank's services is that
   they charge a whopping $10 per transaction. For
   someone who is looking to trade many stocks
   simultaneously, $10 can be pretty steep.

2. **3.Lightning Speed:** The last online brokerage service
   that we'll look at tailors its services in particular to
   people who are trading frequently. Similar to the TD
   thinkorswim platform, Lighting Speed offers to its
   investors a professional help desk staffed with people
   who are investors themselves and professionals in their

field. This type of customer service is available both during normal business hours and after hours as well. While the customer service that Lightning Speed provides is important to their overall image and appeal, it's important to note that their commission fee is one cent more than Interactive Broker's. It's safe to say that if you're looking for a brokerage firm who can offer you advice and you're not that interested in the statistical facts that TD can provide, this might the best route for you to take.

Finding a broker can be described as one of the preliminary steps that you should be taking as you consider day trading. Most of the steps that we discussed in the first chapter of this book had to do with priming your behavior and your mind for day trading, but this is a step that is entirely necessary and can help you to set your investment goals. Failure to find a fair and honest broker can result in the loss of thousands of dollars, depending on how frequently you trade. Before you even start trading, it's a good idea to be actively researching all of the brokerage firms that are available to you. This is certainly not an exhaustive list. Be sure to take the time to compare all brokerage firms that can offer day traders a fair commission price, and most importantly always compare companies against one another.

Chapter 3:

Seven Essential Day Trading Tips for Beginners

If you already have a basic understanding of stock trading in general prior to picking up this book, you can see that broadly speaking, day trading and stock trading are fairly similar. You make sure you have the capital, you find the right broker that fits your needs, and you do the research to make sure that the stocks in which you're looking to trade are going to ultimately prosper. This chapter will focus on the areas of day trading that differ from the broader points of stock trading. The tips presented in this chapter will provide you with concrete ways to increase the likelihood that you'll be successful through the avenue of day trading. Later chapters will focus on specific strategies that you can use to target the day trading market as a whole, and you'll be able to add these nuanced tips to any broad strategy that you ultimately choose to take.

Day Trading Tip 1: Only Purchase Shares when You Have

Money to Burn

One important lesson that all stock traders must take to heart is the idea that they are essentially gambling their money on

the New York Stock Exchange or on another trading floor. The
money that you spend here is potentially money that you're
never going to get back, and you should be purchasing shares
and engaging in trade deals with this in mind. Regular stock
traders at least have the luxury of being able to hold onto a bad
stock to see if it will appreciate over a longer period of time.
This is not the case for day traders. Additionally, many smart
investors have a retirement or savings fund that they're
looking to grow. They keep this money separate from the
money that they're playing on the market. Consider adopting
this sort of mindset. If you do make the decision to trade
money that is from a retirement or savings fund, make sure
that the trade is a fairly conservative one. Often, day trading
does not allow of much conservatism. Keep this in mind as
you decide on how much money to spend.

Along these same lines, recognize that day traders are typically
purchasing many different stocks throughout the day. This
means that you should be spending less money per stock than
you would if you were trading more infrequently. Thinking
about your finances in this manner will force you to begin to
think in the short term rather than in the long term. There's
no reason to purchase an expensive day stock, unless you have
a fair idea that it's going to increase in value by the end of the
day. The last thing that you want, especially as a new day
trader, is for your money to vanish before you even have the
chance to get used to everything that encompasses day
trading.

Day Trading Tip 2: Be Ready to Go!

One of the biggest problems that many beginning day traders
face is actually having the courage to get started. Often, a new
day trader will spend so much time analyzing their potential

stocks and comparing themselves to other traders in the industry that they get cold feet. If you feel yourself acting similarly to the characteristics that were described above, resist the urge to completely back out of day trading altogether. After they've actually started to trade, one of the other problems that some new day traders have is that they spend so much time watching their screens for the right opportunity to present itself that when it does, they don't act decisively enough. Remember our statistic from earlier in the book? Between fifty to seventy-five percent of all day trades take place in a matter of seconds. Stick to your strategy, and if the moment that you should be acting presents itself, make your move. If you end up miscalculating the trade, know that there's something that isn't working in your plan and go back to the drawing board. If you adhere to the first tip that's presented in this chapter and only spend money that you can afford to lose, making a beginner's error won't be that big of a deal anyway.

Day Trading Tip 3: Find your Discipline and Stick to It

Once you have figured out the type of trading plan that you want to be using, it's important that you don't stray from your intentions. Especially when you first begin to day trade, impulses might be able to get the best of you. Even if your instinct is telling that a particular trade is a good idea, you might be going against traditional day trading principles by engaging in the deal. This is why it's important to not only have a mentor or a teacher prior to engaging in day trading, but it's also important to stick to the strategy that you have in place. This is where the emotional and abstract concepts of fear and greed can come into play.

For example, if you were to exit from a deal out of fear even though you know that your strategy is telling you to keep your money in the trade for a bit longer, you are going against your doctrine. If you end up going freestyle and working off of instinct alone, there's a chance that fear will lead you to miss out on a great money-making opportunity. Contrastingly, if your strategy is telling you that it's time to let one of your shares go because the market is taking a turn for the worse, greed might be the little devil that's keeps you from pulling the plug. The result to this type of decision could result in the loss of money that didn't have to be gone if you had simply stuck with what you had learned. Be disciplined and let your strategy be the ultimate deciding factor on which stocks stay and which stocks go.

Day Trading Tip 4: Patience is Always a Virtue

One factor that may turn out to be the most perplexing or surprising for you to find out is that day traders sometimes do not trade every single day. Sometimes, if a day trader is sitting as his or her computer but don't see any opportunities that fit within their strategy, they'll watch the market without doing much at all. Many day traders, when they're first starting out, feel as if they need to constantly be trading at the sake of their better judgement or overall plan that they've implemented. A great mantra that is often heard within the day trading world is one that goes like this: Plan Your Trade, Then Trade Your Plan. Be sure that the trades that you're making fit within the overall structure that you've created for you and your goals, and don't be hasty just because you aren't seeing anything that's worth your trouble.

Day Trading Tip 5: Enter into a Trade when the Supply and the Demand for a Stock are Drastically Imbalanced

If you've ever taken an introduction to economics class (it's likely that you have if you're interested in stock trading), one of the key elements to this type of class is the theory of supply and demand. This theory pertains to the stock market as much as it does the economy as a whole. When demand is high and it seems as if every single investor is looking to purchase a particular stock because it's the "hot" commodity during a given period of time, it's almost guaranteed that the price of this stock is going to rise because of the increase in demand in conjunction with a limited supply of shares. Contrastingly, when demand is low and the market is saturated with shares that seemingly nobody wants, the price of that stock is going to be relatively low. Having this basic sense of what's going on regarding supply and demand within the stock market will provide you with a better ability to track when a particular share is going to increase or decrease in price. All you have to do is track the historical price of the stock over the relatively short period of time and make sure that you're researching the climate of the company when you're looking to buy. For example, if PlayStation 2 was about to unleash a new gaming system on the world, it might be a good idea to purchase a share of this stock as investors prepare for this release. You have a feeling that demand for a PlayStation product is going to be high, so you can also assume that the shares of a PlayStation stock are also going to grow. If you can pinpoint a point in time when the shares of a certain company are going to become more or less saturated with other investors, this will help you to plan accordingly.

Day Trading Tip 6: Set Price Limits Before You Start Trading

Think about it. If you don't set target prices for yourself, how are you going to be able to determine when you should be trading a particular stock? While it sometimes can be okay for a regular stock trader to purchase a particular stock without having a clear notion of exactly how much money he or she is willing to potentially lose, it's at least possible for these types of investors to figure it out over a long period of time. Day traders do not have this luxury.

Before you even get to the point of trading, you should be deciding how much of a profit would be acceptable to you, as well as exactly how much money you're willing to lose on one particular trade. Of course, everyone wants to make as much money as possible through the stock market, but the reality is that there are limits to how much you can make through each transaction, especially when you're partaking in day trading. Instead of going into a trade with the mindset of "I'm going to make tons of money through this deal!" try to push yourself to think about your stocks a bit more rationally. Look at the stock's history and figure out on average how much it has been making for other investors in the past. Then make your decision, and stick to it. It's perhaps even more important to determine how much you're willing to lose on a particular trade before calling it quits. If you set a stopping point for yourself, it's less likely that you'll find yourself in a situation where the stock has plummeting and you're still holding onto the debt remains of its corpse.

Day Trading Tip 7: Understand and Use the Risk-Reward Ratio

Our final day trading tip involves a concept known as the risk-reward ratio. The risk reward ratio, in its most basic sense, means that the ratio that you win from a particular trade should outweigh the risks that are associated with the trade by a certain amount. For day trading in particular, you should be looking to calculate a risk-reward ratio that is 1:3, meaning that the reward associated with the risk is three times greater than any risk that could become a problem. Of course, this ratio is not determined simply through arbitrary means. Instead, the risk-reward can be mathematically determined. When you're looking to figure out the risk-reward ratio, you need to numbers. First, you figure out how much money you as the investor expects to make on the trade. This is your reward, and for our example this number will be considered as N. The other number that you have is the risk, and this is determined by figuring out much you could potentially lose if the stock were to decrease. For our purposes this number will be delineated as r. After you have figured out these two numbers, the calculation is fairly simple and as follows:

$r\ /\ N = Risk\ /\ Reward\ Ratio$

For example, let's say that you are looking to purchase a particular stock of GE and the stock is currently priced at $20 per share. The first step is to figure out how much you are looking to win from this investment. After some deliberation, you decide that you would like to win twenty percent from this investment, and this would mean that the stock would have to increase by four dollars by the end of the day. On the other hand, you have been looking at the recent history of GE stock tendencies and have noticed that the stock, when it's in decline, has been decreasing by at least 1.75 dollars per drop.

In order to figure out the risk to reward ratio, you would make the following calculation:

1.75 / 4 = .4375

In this particular scenario that we've created, it's pretty clear to see that the risk / reward ratio for a stock of GE would not be a good investment for you because the ratio does not result in a reward that's three times greater than the risk. When converted into a fraction, .4375 becomes 7/16, and this means that the risk / reward ratio is closer to fifty-fifty than three times greater for the reward. The picture below can help to clarify this point.

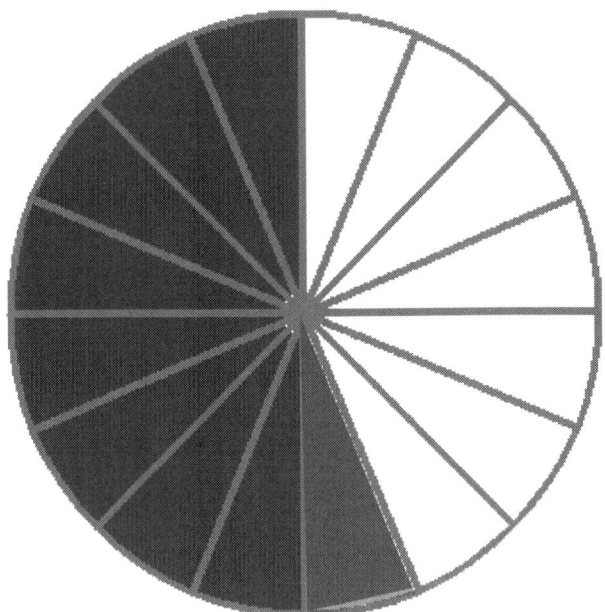

In the picture above, the white blocks represent the risk that is involved, which is seven out of sixteen blocks in total. On the other hand, this means that there are only nine blocks that make up the reward in the trading situation. 7 and 9 are rather close in range, are they not? Their proximity is a good and fast indicator that if you were to purchase a share of GE, you have almost a fifty-fifty chance of losing your money. These are not good odds, especially not for a new day trader.

Overall, if you can learn to follow the tips presented in this chapter, they should be able to provide you with a great deal of help when you're first starting out. A common thread that exists between many of the tips is the need to develop a strategy that not only works, but that will force you to engage in daily disciplinary tasks in order to accomplish a larger goal. Both tactical tips as well as tips that relate to your character have both been presented, and without concentrating on grooming both it's likely that you will often fall short from the day trading tips that you are trying to reach. It's important to combine all of these strategies so that you can develop the best possible outcomes for yourself.

Chapter 4:

Developing Your Target Price

One of the most important factors that you need to be considering does not only pertain to understanding how day trading works as a whole. In addition to developing a concrete strategy for yourself, you also need to be considering how you should be entering and leaving the market. How are you supposed to know when's a good time to enter and when's a good time to exit? This chapter will focus on three key beginner entry strategies that you can use at your disposal. These include learning how to interpret what's known as candlestick charts, understanding level II quotes, and understanding what to take as important from the stock market news. Once you understand what's going on, this type of information will be able to help you know when the market is prime for entry.

Additionally, some of the terms that are presented in this chapter are thrown around in the stock market on a daily basis, and if you're behind on the lingo then you're going to have less of an idea of what's going on. There are far too many day trading terms to be able to condense them all into one chapter. For this reason, be sure to be on the lookout for my advanced guide to day trading that follows this book in sequence.

How to Find a Target Price

Before we take a look at specific strategies that you can be implementing for your day trades, we're going to examine the different types of target prices that you can set for yourself. A target price is the price at which you would ideally want to both sell and purchase a share of a particular stock. There are various ways that you can go about identifying your target price, and deciding on one ultimately is a decision that's made based on your overall trading strategy and style. Of course, you are going to want to have a firm process in which you purchase your stocks, and the different ways to find your target price can help to accomplish exactly that.

Target Price Technique 1: Momentum

The first price targeting technique at which we'll look involves finding "momentum" from news stories and other types of press releases. A common technique that is often used by traders who are implementing momentum involves picking up a stock when a news story about the company is hot, and then trading it when the story takes the company into what is known as "reversal". Reversal just means that the stock is now moving in the opposite direction from what it previously was. Another type of momentum-focused strategy that some traders use involves the price of a particular item. If you remember the example that we used to discuss supply and demand in a market, this type of momentum works similarly to that. As the volume of a product begins to decrease (or rather when the supply is disappearing), the investor knows that it's time to move on to the next trade.

Target Price Technique 2: Daily Pivots

For this technique, the investor will be looking for a sign of reversal in the stock's price throughout the day. The goal of the investor when he or she is using the technique of a daily pivot is to purchase the stock when it's at a low-price point and sell it when it's at a high price point. Seems simple enough, right? In this way, the investor is preying upon the volatility of the market, or rather how much the price of a stock will vary throughout the day. Volatility is typically defined as the measure of the range of the stock's price within a given period of time. The greater the volatility, meaning the greater the difference between the lowest price and the highest price, the more profit (or loss) potential there is.

Target Price Technique 3: Fading

Fading is when the target price is determined based on when investors who were not previously purchasing the stock begin to buy it again. Fading as a concept is closely related to the concept of shorting stocks. Shorting a stock involves purchasing a stock at a high price and then selling it at a lower price than which you originally bought it. After you've sold it at the lower price, you then purchase it again when it's priced higher and make a profit from this difference. Short selling is involved in the technique of fading because as an investor who is using fading, you are basically targeting people who are eager to be in a particular market once more. The types of investors who you are going to attract when you fade include those who were once scared out of the market for a particular share or stock for some reason and those who are early buyers looking to get to a particular market before others see the trend. The types of stocks that people who are using the technique of fading purchase are usually those that are

overbought, because people are eager to pick up these stocks
due to a saturated market.

The notion and implementation of fading can be risky because
if you miscalculate the market, the idea of the short stock can
potentially backfire on you. You'll have sold your shares at a
low price with no hope of seeing a profit in the future. On the
other hand, fading can also be pretty rewarding. You're
essentially preying on people who feel as if they're missing out
on a hot market, but the advantages to this method certainly
outweigh the potential ethical discrepancies. Remember, the
stock market is a cut-throat kind of place. Any way that you
can get ahead, without cheating, is fair game.

Target Price Technique 4: Scalping

If you've ever been to a baseball game and have seen people
standing on the street selling after-market tickets, then you
have already been acquainted with the notion of scalping.
Scalpers at sporting events are trying to make a profit any way
that they can, and their ultimate goal is to walk away with any
type of profit that they can. Moving back towards the stock
market, when a day trader uses the strategy of scalping, he or
she is looking for any profit that exists. The strategy here is
pretty simple. As soon as the investor sees even the smallest
profit emerge on the market, he or she sells the stock
immediately. This particular strategy is especially popular
amongst day traders because of the fact that it's pretty easy to
implement. As a day trader, you're going to have a bunch of
stocks that you are going to be watching all the time. Instead
of looking at complicated charts and trying to figure out if
you're making the right decision, the technique of scalping can
help you to eliminate any of that. Additionally, scalping is
great because it can disassociate the investor from becoming

too emotionally invested in any one stock. Instead of purchasing a stock and desperately hoping that it will grow astronomically, taking any gain from a stock even when it's small will help you to stay emotionally unattached.

Chapter 5:

Using Candlestick Charts as Part of Your Strategy

ow that you're aware of the general entry strategies that day traders use when they're thinking about purchasing or selling a stock, this next chapter will dig even deeper into strategies that you can develop in order to meet your day trading goals. Understanding the entry strategies that you can use will help you to figure out how to navigate the market once your overall market strategy has been configured. Additionally, it's important to note that "strategy" here means how an investor figures out what he or she is going to purchase next. The craziness of the stock market is mostly due to the fact that nobody truly knows for certain what is going to happen next. For this reason, multiple strategies on how to day trade have been developed. They all work sometimes, and then all fail at other times. That is the nature of the market. Your job is to pick out which strategies appeal to you the most, and then use then as much or as little as you'd like.

What the Heck is a Candlestick Charts

A candlestick chart is a chart that's used in the stock market to gauge how money is moving throughout the day. The picture

below of a candlestick chart should be able to provide you with
a better explanation of how it works.

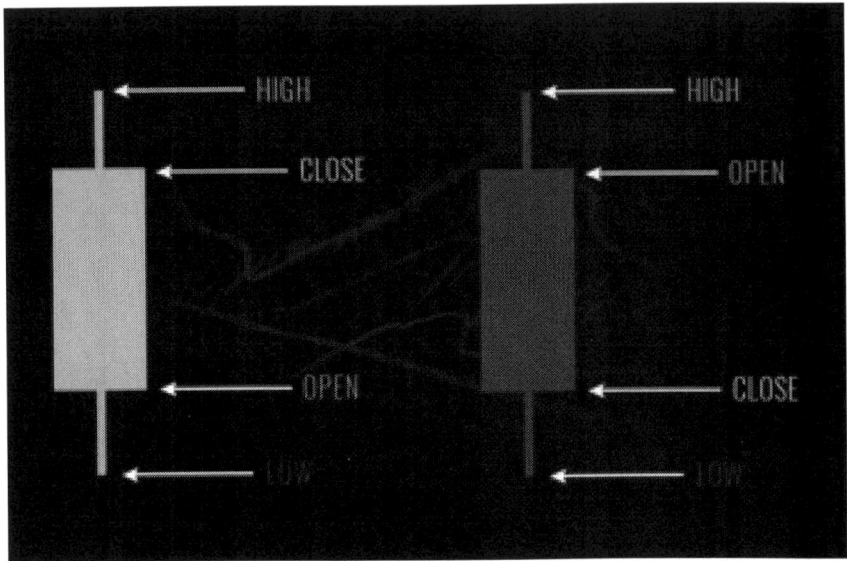

Can you see from the picture how the candlestick chart
received its name? As you can see from the example above,
the color of the candlesticks reveal whether or not the stock is
in the red or in the green, respectively. The tip of the candle,
where the candle would be burning if it were actually a candle
and not a chart, indicates the highest price point for that stock
on a given day. If you look at the green candle, the "Close"
indicator there tells you where the price was at when the stock
market opened. It should be obvious that a green-colored
candle indicates that this stock closed higher than its opening
price, and it's colored red if the stock closed lower than its
opening price. If you look to the bottom of the green candle,
you should be able to see that the "Open" arrow is pointing to
the spot where the stock opened at the beginning of the day.
The "Low" portion of the candle below the word "Open" is able
to show you the price when the stock was at its lowest price

throughout the day. The only difference between the red and green candlesticks that are shown above is that the opening and closing prices are at opposite ends of the graph. One other difference that you might see in some of the candlesticks charts at which you look is the fact that they are usually either filled in with black or left open.

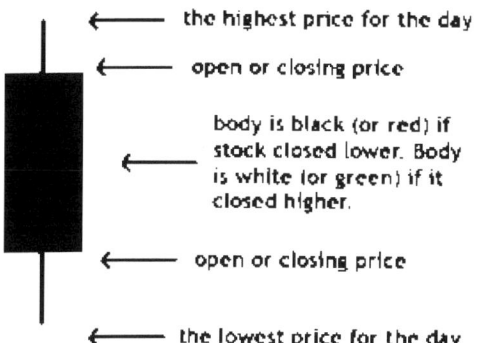

the highest price for the day

open or closing price

body is black (or red) if stock closed lower. Body is white (or green) if it closed higher.

open or closing price

the lowest price for the day

As is evident, this candlestick is not filled in with a green or red color; instead, it's filled in with black, meaning that the closing price at which the stock is set was lower than the price on which it opened. On the other hand, when the candlestick is not filled in at all, this means that the stock closed at a higher price than which it opened. One other factor that is important when seeking to understand the candlestick chart is that the length of the actual body of the candlestick can also help you to figure out how well a stock is doing. For example, when the length of the candlestick is long, this means that the market is going through a "bearish" period. When the stock market is bearish, this means that for one reason or another a lot of pessimism exists in the market. Maybe a particular economic decision has just been passed or a new government official is taking over and is causing a lot of widespread doubt. These are the types of reasons why a market would be bearish, and this results in a mass selling of stock.

Contrastingly, if a market is particularly bullish, this is
basically the opposite of a bearish market. For whatever
reason, no one is selling their stocks, and this can create a
situation where stocks are priced higher than usual. Instead of
being black, these lines will appear as long and white. This
make sense. If no one is selling their stock, the price of the
stocks would appear stagnant, and you'd end up with higher
overall prices. When it's a bearish market and people want to
get out fast, it's likely that the price of the stock will drop due
to the desperate nature of the stock market. When it's a
bearish market, investors are more likely to feel like the stocks
are going to plummet, and they'll want to get out while they
can. For reasons such as this, they'll be more likely to drop
their selling prices in exchange for an overall feeling of
security. The picture below can help to better illustrate to you
the concepts of bullish and bearish markets.

The Shadows of a Candlestick Chart

One other aspect of the candlestick chart is what's known as the "shadow". We have already discussed the shadows briefly. They are the wicks of the candles that protrude from either end of its body. These too, just like the body of the candle, can differ in size. When the shadow is short and is paired with a body that is filled in with black, this means that when the stock market opened, this share was closer to its highest point for the day than when the day was done. When the shadow is short and the body of the candle is white or gray, this means that when the stock closed it was near its high for the day. As you can see from the chart above, the candlesticks on the candlestick chart can vary greater from one another in size, shape, color, and length.

The Notion of a Spinning Top

You can see the phrase "spinning top" etched into the chart that's found above. A spinning top is added to a chart when the difference between the amount of times the stock has been traded between the open and close price is somewhat neutral. These can be found to be either black or white, depending on the preferences of the person or group who creates the chart, and are typically much smaller than most of the lines that exist on the chart.

Doji Lines

The last type of structure that exists on the graph about which we'll discuss is known as the doji line. This type of line can also be seen on the graph that is located above. The doji line can show the investor periods of time when the opening and closing prices for a particular stock were almost exactly the same. This is the smallest figure that will exist on the graph, with the spinning top being the second smallest element.

After learning about the ins and outs of candlestick chart, it should be fairly easy to see how you can start using this tool for your overall strategic goals. The candlestick chart is used by thousands of day traders and even other types of investors so that they can keep track of the closing and opening prices for a stock in which they're interested. If you think back to the concept of a reversal, it is fairly easy to pinpoint on a candlestick chart when a stock might be taking a turn for the better or for the worse. If you combine your study of the candlestick chart with any of the target price strategies that we discussed in the previous chapter, then you should have no trouble figuring out at what point is the right time to enter and leave the market.

Chapter 6:

How to Subscribe to a Level II Quotes Service

If you are thankful for the information that was presented in the previous chapter, but you're still a bit unsure about your own capacity to understand all of the aspects that a candlestick chart can offer, you're certainly not alone. If instead of navigating a chart all by your lonesome, you're looking for something a bit more comprehensive, then it might be a good idea to look at Level II. At its core, Level II is the book of orders that Nasdaq receives each day. Nasdaq is able to turn this complicated and copious amount of information into something succinct and comprehensive for you. As a day trader, this is an extremely useful tool. This chapter will look at exactly how Level II works, as well as the advantages that exist for its users.

How Level II Works

It should be obvious to you by now that there are many different ways that you can purchase a stock, and sometimes it may seem like all of these transactions are all jumbled together and in no distinct order. Level II seeks to add some clarity to this confusion. Not only does Level II provide you with a list of all of the orders that have been placed on the stock market for a given day, it will also rank these for you in order from the best bid and ask prices to the worst. This way, you are able to easily see which investors are making the best deals. For a day trader, this can be extremely useful. Below is a picture of what the format typically looks like within Level II:

Copyright © 2006 Investopedia.com

If we start from the left and work our way towards the right, we can see that the company UBS Securities has ordered five thousand shares of a stock at the price of $102.50. It's important to note here that the "50" does not mean that they are only purchasing 50 shares of stock. Instead, the number of shares in level II terminology means that this amount is multiplied by one hundred. This would mean that if you were looking to purchase only fifty shares instead of five thousand, the number of shares would read ".5". Lastly, instead of cents being documented as decimals, as they are traditionally, Level II instead has them as fractions for whatever reason.

Understanding Your Market

If you recall, in the beginning of this book we discussed how it's important to understand your market before you start day trading. Level II can help you to do just that. Within Level II's list, each investor who is participating on the stock market also has an abbreviated word in a column that's marked "Market". For example, if you were looking at a particular list and saw that one of them said "MSCO", you would know that this investor used the company Morgan Stanley to purchase their shares. Additionally, there are three types of investor types that all play on the same trading platform with which you should be familiar. They are:

- **Market Makers (MM):** Market Makers are the investors who give liquidity to the stock market as a whole. These are the players who make the stock market run, because without them there would be no market as we know it. These market makers are forced to purchase and sell stock even when no one else is buying or selling. As market makers, it's their duty.

- **Electronic Communications Networks (ECN):** Electronic Communication Networks are what make it possible place orders online and through a computer. As the world gets faster and faster, it can seem like ECNs are the way that increasingly numbers of people are looking to invest, and for a day trader an ECN is not a bad option because it can generally close deals faster than physical people can.

- **Wholesalers (Order Overflow):** This type of service allows brokerage firms to sell the orders that they've promised to fill to outside vendors who will fill the orders instead of the original broker. If you own a business and have ever used a subcontractor for a service that you want to provide to your customer but do not actually perform the work yourself, then you pretty much already know how a wholesaler works. One of the reasons why brokers turn to wholesalers at all is because sometimes brokers bite off more than they can chew. If they are struggling to fulfill all of the

orders that they receive, the wholesaler route is the
perfect one to take.

The Advantages to Using Level II Quotes

There are many advantages that exist when you take the time
to invest in Level II Quotes. One of the biggest ones is that you
can tell a lot about not just the climate of the market as a
whole but also the type of buying that is going on. When you
analyze the types of markets that are contributing to the
market, you might be able to see larger patterns that can lead
you to a conclusion of some type. Additionally, if you look for
irregularities within the ECN orders, you might be able to
figure out when bigger institutional players on the stock
market are trying to be sneaky in their selling and purchasing
tactics. If you see these types of patterns, it could mean that a
merger or another type of big event is going to be taking place
for the company. Lastly, you can figure out when a trend
might be coming to an end by looking at the trades that are
taking place between the bid price and the asking price. When
a big trend is coming to a close, one of the surest ways to figure
this out is to look for big traders who are choosing to take a
small loss in order to escape from the stock before it
plummets. Think about it. Why would someone be willing to
take a loss on a stock if their only alternative was to take an
even bigger loss later down the line? If you see an influential
trader taking a loss on a hot stock, it's most likely time to jump
ship when them and get out while you still can.

Risks Associated with Level II Quotes

Of course, every type of strategy can have risks associated with
it, although it can be argued that it's difficult to find risks for
using the candlestick chart when trading because that

mechanism is fairly safe in quality. It's hard to find discrepancies that exist for an empirical chart. Anyway, back to Level II Quotes. Because big investors know that little guys like you and me will be scrutinizing their activity through Level II Quotes, they will often try to play tricks on the application. Some other types of deceptive tricks that large investors will use include the following:

Placing Smaller Orders: One of the biggest ways that market makers hide their large orders is by placing smaller orders and updating their numbers whenever they fill an order through a sale. The primary motivation for market makers to do this is because if they were to unleash their entire arsenal of shares on the market at once, it would likely scare many investors away from purchasing their stock. Some investors might even leave the market altogether.

Deception through the Short Sale: Remember the short sale that we discussed in a previous chapter? Well sometimes big and influential investors will use the short sale against the smaller investor. What they'll do is offer a large sum of money to someone who is interested in short selling, only to cancel the order later on and bid a large sum of money instead. Unless the investor is also a day trader, he or she may not see the large bid until it's too late, and they'll end up losing money on the whole thing. If the investor does see the large big, he or she is forced by the bigger fish in the market to work overtime in order to make sure that they're money is safe. Like I said before, sometimes day trading can be rather cut-throat if you're not careful.

Deception Through ECNs: Lastly, market makers are also known to use electronic networks to make their transactions, with the knowledge that ECNs can be used by anyone within the stock market. While the Level II Quotes allow you to see

how the investor is trading, it does not allow you to see
whether the investor is an institutional one who is backed by a
large corporation, or a smaller retail vendor. Due to this fact,
it can sometimes be hard for an investor to tell when they're
being taken advantage of by an entity that's bigger than
themselves.

When thinking about Level II Quotes in its entirety, know that
it can truly be a great resource for learning more about your
market and what the trading climate is like. On the other
hand, it is also a highly distrustful place. The discussion above
should prove to you that you can never be sure of what
experienced and savvy investors are trying to convey over
Level II Quotes. Instead of using this method exclusively, it's
advised that you use it in conjunction with another strategy of
your choosing. This will provide you with the reinforcements
that your investments need in order to make sure that the
decisions that you're making are backed by fact rather than
backed by hope, desire, or loftiness.

Chapter 7:

Additional Resources at Your Disposal

While I certainly hope that this book has helped you get the gist of what day trading is and how it works, the simple reality is that you should seek further education before jumping into the day trading market. Remember, day trading is not a cheap endeavor. The last thing that you want to do to yourself is jump into the day trading waters and lose your shirt before you even know which end is up. Thus, there are countless other resources that you should be considering before you start day trading right away.

Consider Formal Day Trading Education

The fact of the matter is if you're going to get serious about day trading, you're going to want to have specific facts about the type of stocks that you're looking to invest your money into, as well as these specific processes. Of course, textbooks cost little money in comparison to the price of many of the stocks that you're going to be trading, and there are other books that exist on the web that can also get you to where you need to be so that you can start trading comprehensively.

Consider a Mentor

If reading constantly just isn't for you, you should also consider hiring a mentor. What's even better than hiring a mentor is finding someone with whom you're close who can provide you with information and more importantly experience. Ask this person if you can spend a day with them while they day trade, and try to learn how it works from this nuanced and complex perspective. If you're actually in the game, watching it be done, this will give you a better idea of how you need to act once you start trading for yourself.

Consider Webinars

Another potential idea that you should be thinking about implementing for yourself is finding an academy online. Depending on what you can find, online courses can sometimes cost as little as a couple hundred dollars. What's great about an official online course is that you are often able to finish this at your leisure, without the formality of a formal classroom setting. Of course, if you're serious about day trading and you want to get started as quickly as possible, you'll finish the course in no time at all. Often, these courses will also provide you with tutors or teachers who will be guiding you every step of the way.

Conclusion

Thank for making it through to the end of *Day Trading: A Crash Course to Get Quickly Started and Make Immediate Cash in Only One Day of Trading,* let's hope it was informative and able to provide you with all of the tools you need to achieve your goals whatever it may be. Now you should have a comprehensive understanding of what day trading is, how you can starting doing it for yourself, and most importantly how you can make money in just one day! The information presented in this book was designed so that you can go out and start trading immediately as a beginner; however, if you are interested in learning everything that you can about the topic of day trading before you start actually doing it, then you should be on the lookout for my other book that's about day trading! It's as informative as this book was, but instead of being filled with information for beginners it's geared towards folks who have been day trading for a little while or people who are looking to expand their knowledge to the fullest extent possible before they get into the nitty gritty of day trading. Regardless of which type of situation you find yourself, that book could be for you!

The next step is to keep progressing towards a place where you feel comfortable day trading on your own. Rent books on the topic from the library, find mentors who you know personally, and always look to the internet to push your breadth of knowledge even further than it already exists at. We do live in the information age, after all. Remember that the internet can

provide you not only with information, but also with new
communication networks. Sources like LinkedIn and online
forums can help you to connect with experts in the field who
are ready and eager to provide free information to you.
Additionally, you can always find ways to pay astronomical
sums of money in exchange for advice, but you should look to
the free avenues first. As is the case with most stock market
investment strategies, there is no hard and fast rule when it
comes to the right strategies. Everyone forges their own path;
however, many people and companies that exist on the
internet will use their influential marketing tools to persuade
you to think otherwise. They'll have you believe that day
trading is all about a specific process and steps, and they'll
teach you these steps at an expensive rate. Don't fall for this
kind of ploy. Take the risks and learn for yourself. You'll be
glad you did at the end of the day.

Finally, if you found this book useful in anyway, a review on
Amazon is always appreciated!

DAY TRADING:

The Best Techniques To Multiply Your Cashflow In Only One Day Of Trading

By Samuel Rees

Introduction

Welcome to the exciting world of day trading! If you're here, you are looking for concrete tips and techniques to making money on the stock market. Day trading is fast-paced and risky, as you know. It takes great instincts and an iron will, but it also absolutely needs a plan. Strategy and a cool head are what separate the wheat from the chaff here. This book will teach you not only about the various methods day traders use, but how to choose which ones are right for your goals and how to utilize them effectively. Finally, we'll look at some of the common pitfalls day traders encounter and how to avoid them.

Overcoming Taxes and Commissions

E ven using a discount broker, you will have to pay a fee on every trade you make. Add in the taxes you'll have to pay on any profit and you'll see that day trading can be quite an expensive proposition. This means that in order to come out on top, you're going to have to earn quite a bit more than you may think at first. Conversely, you should be mindful from day one to keep your commissions down as much as possible. After all, the less you pay out, the less you have to make back up with profitable trades.

A very simple but common mistake that novice day traders make is not calculating both the entry and exit fees for their trades. Think of your trades as round-trip plane tickets. After all, the trade isn't complete until you've "arrived at your destination," i.e., you've exited the market, hopefully having turned a profit.

It's important to think of commissions not in dollar amounts, but in percentages of trade profits. For example, if the broker charges a fee of $10, giving you a "round-trip" fee of $200. On a trade where your calculations stand to give you a profit of $10,000, this isn't a problem, as the fees only amount to .2% of profits. If, however, your trade has a potential value of only $100, the fee will end up being a whopping 20% of your profit.

DAY TRADING: The Best Techniques To Multiply Your Cashflow In Only One Day Of Trading

This is an extreme example obviously, but it illustrates how different the meaningful value of $20 can be.

Some brokers offer special terms that may be of particular benefit to high-volume traders. For instance, they may discount fees for traders who make more than a certain amount of trades per month. There are also brokers who charge a set annual fee on the assets the broker is managing in total. This removes the importance of the number of trades you make in a month because the fee doesn't change.

Whichever circumstance you have with your broker, it's important to calculate the fees when planning trades. As you'll see in the coming chapters, preparation is the best part of victory for the day trader. You'll spend a good amount of time researching securities, scouring the market for entry and exit points, and setting up orders to act quickly and protect you from loss. You'll need to build commission calculation into this process so that when the market opens and you are trading in real time it doesn't slip your mind.

There is a common conception that day traders are constantly making trades, day in and day out. This isn't the case, and if it were, commission fees would quickly eat up all the profits. As long as you're drawing your parameters for trades appropriately, you'll limit their number and by doing so limit the commissions you will be charged.

Taxes are a bear for any trader, but for the day trader they can be especially difficult. Traders and investors are treated differently by the tax code but the defining line between the two isn't clear. You'll need to determine if you meet the definition of a trader in order to take advantage of the self-employed status traders enjoy. If you do meet the standard for a trader, you'll be able to deduct things like your home computer and office space. The tax code limits which kinds of losses are acceptable to write off, and to what limit. You'll need to keep careful records in order to figure out what you bought when. It is absolutely critical not to leave your tax preparation until the last minute. Ideally, you should be filing taxes and withholding your own deductions quarterly in order to avoid a big bill at the end of the fiscal year. There are many software options for tracking this. It is definitely worth your time to find one that works for you and use it religiously.

Charts and Analysis

Reading and Using Candlesticks

Candlesticks are used to quickly display the movement of a stock over a time period, usually a day. You'll frequently see candlesticks strung together to represent longer periods of time. Understanding how to read them and what their information can tell you about the probable movement of the stock is crucial. Before you begin day trading you'll need to be able to read these like a piano player reads music. If you have to stop and figure out what means what, you'll miss opportunities left and right.

Here are the basic parts of a candlestick chart and what they represent-

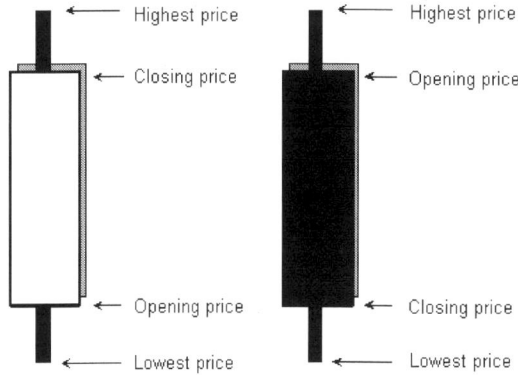

The rectangular (or sometimes square portion) of the chart is called the body. The lines on the top and bottom are called the upper and lower shadows. A white bar means that the closing price was higher than the opening price on that day. A colored-in bar means the opposite; the closing price was lower than the opening price. In other words, A white bar means the stock price rose on that day, and a black (sometimes red or other colors are used) bar means the stock price fell on that day.

The lengths of the shadows and heights of the bodies show us the difference in the openings and closings and the lows and highs throughout the day.

Because candlesticks pack so much information into one chart, traders have named several of the common chart patterns to provide a kind of shorthand for their meaning. The chart was first used in the 18th century in Japan, so quite a few of the names come from Japanese. It might take a while to develop familiarity with them, but it's worth the effort. Keep in mind that in the following descriptions there will be small amounts of variation within each definition. For example, a hammer might have no lower shadow at all but might have a small one. Both would be correct examples of a hammer. Another important thing to note is the meaning of the words "positive" and "negative" in these definitions. They don't mean "good" or "bad," but rather "upwardly trending in price" and "downwardly trending in price," respectively. Depending on your investment strategy, a price downturn might be great for you.

One Day Patterns

White Marubozu- This chart looks almost like a bar. It has no (or very little) shadow on either end. This is a positive signal meaning that the daily high of the stock price is very close to the closing price, and the daily low is very close to the opening price. When there is a bit of shadow on either end it's known as a "big white body."

Black Marubozu- A black marubozu holds the opposite meaning to the white marubozu, and it looks just the same except for the color of the body. This is a strongly negative symbol. It means that the highest price of the day was very close to the opening price and the lowest price was close to the closing price. So, during the trading day, the stock has lost value. When there is a bit of shadow on either end it's known as a "big black body."

Opening Marubozu- In a candlestick chart with a white body, this will look like an actual candle. It will have almost no bottom shadow, a long white body, and a tall upper shadow (also called a wick.) This means that the opening price and the lowest price of the day were close to one another and that the closing price and high price of the day were somewhat far apart, but that the stock is still doing well. It is considered a positive sign. A black opening marubozu will look like the opposite: a long black bar very near the top of the chart with a long shadow below (also called the tail.) This means that the opening price and the highest price of the day were near one another and that the closing price was not the lowest of the day, but it wasn't drastically higher than the lowest. It is a sign of negative movement.

Closing Marubozu- Closing marubozu look like the inverse of their opening counterparts. They carry the same meanings, but their difference is one of degree. While an opening white marubozu signals a somewhat-positive movement, a closing white marubozo is even more positive. A black closing marubozu is therefore even more of a negative-direction signal than an opening one.

Doji- A Doji is a candlestick that represents a very close opening and closing price so that the body is a line (or nearly a line).

$$\dagger$$

Dragonfly Doji- This candlestick looks like a capital letter T and may signal an upcoming reversal.

Doji Star- This looks like a lowercase letter t and may signal an upcoming reversal.

Four Price Doji- This looks like just a dash (-) with no shadow above or below the body. It usually signals an upcoming reversal.

Hammer/Hanging Man- This is looks like a square lollipop, with a short body fully at the top of the chart, no wick, and a long tail. In a downwardly trending market it is called a hammer, and it signals an upturn. In a bullish (upwardly trending) market, it is called a hanging man and signals a reversal downward.

Inverted Hammer- This is the opposite of a Hammer. It will look like a square at the bottom of a long string. The body will be short and fully at the bottom of the chart with a long wick at the top. A white body signals a weakening rising power and a black body signals a rising falling power. In other words, it is a sign of a reversal in the amount of movement.

Two Day Patterns

Harami- This is a combination of two candlesticks, one being a large body and the second being a smaller body of the opposite color or a doji. If the second chart is a doji, it is called a Harami Cross.

Bearish Harami- This is represented by a large white body followed by a small black bodied chart. It signals an upward movement when it appears following an uptrend in the stock's price history.

Bearish Harami Cross- This is represented by a large white body followed by a doji. It signals a reversal.

Bullish Harami- This is represented by a large black body followed by a much smaller white body. In the context of a downtrend, it usually signals upward movement.

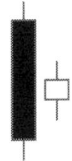

Bullish Harami Cross- This is represented by a large black body followed by a doji. It signals a reversal.

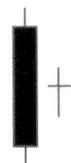

Windows- A window is a gap between the bottom of the body of the first candlestick and the top of the body of the next. This can mean different things depending on the individual charts and the amount of distance between them. Note that some patterns function in the same way as windows, just to lesser degrees, when there is some overlap.

Falling Window- This is represented by a black body candlestick side-by-side with a white body candlestick, with the bottom of the black body being above the top of the white body. The gap in between the bottom of the first and the top of the second is the window. The level of the window represents the resistance. Resistance is a concept we'll explore further later, but it means the high-watermark price that the stock is tending to top out at.

Rising Window- This is represented by two white bodied candlesticks with the top of the first below the bottom of the second. This means that second-day low was above the first-day high. The window is a signal of the support, meaning the low-watermark price the stock tends to bottom out at. Again, the concept of support is slightly more complicated than this, but we'll address that in later chapters.

On Neckline- This is a black body candlestick and a small body white candlestick together. In a downtrending context, this signals a bearish pattern, especially if the bottom of the black body intersects the top of the white body.

There are also three and four day patterns, and you'll frequently see entire months and quarters mapped out with candlesticks. Spend time studying the charts and you'll see many patterns emerge. These patterns will be the key to your ability to quickly understand market forces and react to them.

Level II Quotes

Level II quotes are one of the most important tools in your day trading toolbox. They are very time sensitive, so they give you one of the most up-to-date pictures of what the market is really doing in real time. You'll need to be very comfortable reading them and interpreting the information contained in them instantly.

Looking at a level II is basically looking at the NASDAQ orders from all of the players in the market. Think of it like a diner. At one table you have the Market Makers. These are broker-dealer firms that intentionally maintain liquidity in the market by selling shares when orders are placed in order to be the first to supply the orderer with the requested shares. The next table is full of robots; those are ECNs. These are Electronic

Communications Networks. ECNs are automated order fulfillment services that function online. They're "controlled" by all kinds of people and entities, from individual brokers all the way up to the biggest investment houses. At the last table are wholesalers.

Wholesalers are the brass-tacks order fillers who are usually doing the work assigned to them by someone else. Discount brokers frequently contract the actually trading work to wholesalers.

Looking at a level II is not just like looking at the whole restaurant at once, it's like looking at the waiter's order pad from all three tables.

A level II stock quote is displayed as a four letter code representing the player investing, a number representing the price they are paying for the stock, and finally, a number representing the number (in hundreds) of shares they are buying. Here's an example:

ABCD 220 20

This would mean, for example, that market maker ABCD had bought 2,000 shares of the given stock for $220 per share.

If you watch the level II on a given stock for a few days, you'll usually find that one player is dominating the price. This player is called "the Ax." Their buying price will mirror the average high trading price for the stock. It's usually advisable to trade the stock with the ax, because they are not only a predictor of the stock price, but the driver of it.

Just knowing the general trends of a stock is clearly not enough, though. If it were, you could use other information, like candlesticks, to tell you that. So what else can looking at a level II do for you? Quite a bit, it turns out. For example, you can see whether the orders being placed are retail or institutional. This can give you insight into who is interested in the stock, and you can determine from there if that data strengthens or weakens the stock value in your eyes. You can also look for market makers trying to fake the resistance level. If you see a market maker placing multiple small bids well below the resistance level you've detected through your other research, this means that they know the resistance is surmountable, but they're trying not to tip their hands to other traders.

Daily Pivots

You'll frequently hear about "pivot points" in day trading. These are markers of support and resistance, so it's important to understand what they mean and how they're useful to you in predicting shifts and reversals. Since this is done by every major analyst based on a formula, you don't really need to calculate the pivot points yourself, but it is helpful to understand what they are, how they're formulated, and what they say about support and resistance levels. Depending on your trading strategy, pivots may be of the highest importance to your earnings. If this is the case, make sure you are aware of as many pivot calculations as possible and you seek out plenty of other factors that contribute to reversals so you can ascertain the reliability of the pivot calculation.

How Pivot Points Are Formulated

Pivots points are usually calculated with daily averages or totals but can be calculated with hourly, half-hourly, or even 15-minute information. Most traders stick with the daily pivot point and then apply that to the more finely-sliced charts they use for fast moving trades. The pivot point is a function of the previous day's high and low, and the current day's opening price. The formula looks like this: ((Today's opening price x 2) + Yesterday's Low + Yesterday's High) /4. From that number, different support and resistance levels are calculated. There are other formulas that can be used, but this is the most common.

The resistance and support levels that come from this are referred to as S1, S2, S3 and R1, R2, R3.

Using Pivot Points in Daily Trading

There are two ways to use these data points. First, they are useful in identifying market trends. When they break upward, the market is moving the same way. The opposite is true as well. This is a valuable indicator of trends within a day because most trend tracking only works in the context of multiple days.

Next, they can be used to plan entry and exit points in the market. For instance, a stop loss can be triggered when the price meets a certain resistance level because that is an indicator that a momentum shift is occurring.

Decoding News and Analysis

For the purposes of day trading, traditional research and analysis methods are simply too slow to be effective. You'll need more than thorough research and valuations if you expect to trade as quickly and efficiently as you'll need to. Because of this, you'll need to keep a close eye on expert analysis and the comings-and-goings of the companies you're interested in trading in. You'll have to do this not just with an eye toward the long-term prospects of the companies. You'll need to be able to critically understand how seemingly minute movements in share prices within short-term histories will affect your goals.

Macro Sites

These are analysis sites that take a more global view of the stock market. While you're obviously not going to be able to pick any individual stocks based on the information on a site like this, learning about the wider context of the market is wonderfully grounding when you are making your actual trades. Additionally, you'll be able to see industries and types of funds that seem to emerge from the mass and make themselves just a little more visible. This is a sign to take a closer look, to dial in your analysis.

Look at Patterns

Decontextualized information is always misleading, but in the case of stock information, this is particularly true. This applies to analysis just as much as it does to market behavior itself. When scouting a site or company to provide analysis, spend some time watching how well their predictions track with what actually ends up happening. Pay attention to how well your goals match up with the values of the analysis. These things don't have to (and never will) map perfectly one-to-one, but you should look for a close match in both accuracy and shared values.

Don't make the common mistake of thinking that you are able to do all the analysis from raw data on your own. There is simply too much information out there and you need your energy for decision-making. You'll have quite a bit of parsing to do even with the help of pros. Don't double your energy output in this area because it absolutely won't increase your effectiveness.

Spot the Intra-Day Trends

Once you've found news sources and analysts that you are comfortable with and trust, look at their treatment of intra-day trends as well as inter-day ones. You'll start to see patterns emerge in the hours between the market's opening and close. Look for hours with more movement than usual other than the first hour after opening. It's important to become comfortable with the ebb and flow of the market well before you jump in so that you're never taken by surprise by the fluctuations that occur every day, sometimes by the minute.

Strategies and Techniques

Now that you have the ability to analyze stock microhistories, buyer trends, and the market forces affecting both of these, you're ready to choose the strategies that you'll use to engage with the market. There are several styles of day trading, and you'll probably want to utilize some or most of them depending on the situation. That's why it's important that you understand all of them, so that when you are making the quick pivots that the market requires, you're ready.

It is incredibly helpful to spend time with a stock market simulator executing these trades repeatedly before jumping into the actual market. A day or two won't be enough; you'll need to accumulate hundreds of hours of practice before you're ready to put real money on the line. Don't rush the preparation stage. While traditional investing may move slow enough to allow you to recover from errors, day trading isn't, so you'll need to have the instincts to avoid those errors, at least most of the time.

Fades

A fade is the practice of buying a falling stock that you expect to bottom out and reverse soon, and when it does, selling it for the higher, rebounding price. It takes a strong stomach to execute this because you're moving in the opposite direct from the market. If you got your start in traditional, long-term trading this will feel intensely counterintuitive. This strategy is inherently high-risk because if the market doesn't bottom out where you think it will you're going to lose money. Or, if you hold onto it too long after the rebound hoping to make a little more than your target, it could fall again. On the other hand, it is very profitable when it works, as you're in the position of not only holding a stock that everyone suddenly wants to buy, you can influence its value by setting the offer.

There are some strategies that can make fading safer than blind guessing and intuition though.

Measuring Against Past Performance

First off, many experts have had great success by looking at the stock's performance at the same time the previous year to predict trends. This obviously won't apply to every stock, but many are seasonal in nature. This can help you differentiate between movement that is continuous and movement that is heading toward a reversal. Make sure to fully study the context of the previous year's information, though. Check news from the surrounding weeks to make sure that it was, in fact, market forces at work and not a special event like a buyout or launch that affected the price.

Opening Fades

Opening Fades are fades done soon after the stock market opens, usually within the first hour. This might be the least stressful of all the fade tactics (which certainly doesn't mean it's stress-free) because you're able to take a bit of time to research your trades and prepare your orders before the trading day begins. Then, when the market opens, you either let your pre-set orders take effect or watch the market and pull the trigger when you hit your target. At this point you can either keep trading, possibly switching tactics, or that can be your trading day.

Fading the Gap

The gap, if you remember your candlesticks, is the difference between the closing price one day and the opening price the next. Fading the gap involves buying a stock that you believe has gapped for reasons that won't last, and profiting when it moves to be more in line with your expectation. An example can illustrate this more clearly: Say you see that stock XYZ has closed at $10 per share on Tuesday, but opens Wednesday at $20. This rise is based on the previous year's strong earnings, but you happen to know that the company isn't doing nearly as well as it was at this time last year. Therefore, you believe that as the day progresses the stock's price will fall. You short 100 shares of the stock, and when you are proven correct and the stocks do fall in price, you've turned a profit.

The opposite is also an example of fading the gap. Say that stock ABC closed at $50 per share, but that evening news came out that their highly-anticipated product launch is going to be delayed. The next day, they open at $40 per share due to this news. However, you think that the company is fundamentally sound and that when they do launch the product it will be as profitable as it was before the delay. You then "fade the gap" by buying the stock at its lower price and waiting for it to rise as the market catches up to you.

Scalping

Scalping is a technique based on the premise that the less time you spend in the market, the less risk you expose yourself to. And this is absolutely true, but in order for trades with ultraquick turnarounds to be profitable, you need to make a lot of them. A good way to visualize the difference between scalping and traditional trading is to imagine throwing a sponge into a swimming pool. In the first couple of seconds only a small amount of water is going to be absorbed. If you yank it out right away, you're not getting much water. If you leave it in for a whole day, it will become completely saturated, so that when you pull it out you'll get much more water. Scalping is like throwing a hundred sponges in and then pulling them out after a few seconds. Yes, each sponge has only a bit of water, but it adds up.

Now imagine the water is infested with sharks. These represent risk. If you only have one big sponge to throw in and leave it there, maybe the sharks will miss it and it will be fine. If the sharks do eat it, though, there goes your water. If you toss in 100 smaller sponges and the sharks eat a few, you're probably still going to get a decent amount of water at the end of the day. Since your sponges are only in the water for a short amount of time, the sharks aren't going to have much time to snap them up. So you see, scalping works like diversification by spreading risk around as well as mitigating it by limiting exposure.

Scalping Styles

Scalpers fall into two categories: primary and supplementary. (This is true for many styles. It's very common to combine techniques in order to tailor your strategy to all of the factors that affect your trading goals.) Primary scalpers make up to and upwards of 100 small trades a day. Supplementary scalpers may use this technique to supplement traditional day trading or as part of their day trading strategy. Scalping can even be used on the very same stock that a trader has bought with traditional tactics in mind. What would that look like? First, a decent-sized order would be placed on stock that you think is going up soon and for the long-term future. Then, (anticipating the rise that, in part, your purchase is helping to cause), you'll identify setups in that stock that are trending upwards in small time frames. You would typically buy a large amount of shares and then sell them off after small increases have been made.

Setting Targets

Most traders set a target with a 1:1 risk to reward ratio. This is fairly basic, but worth repeating and illustrating here, as knowing your risk to reward ratio is crucial to any trade, but it becomes exponentially more important when you're trading as quickly and frequently as you will be as a scalper. When you identify a setup and initiate a position, you'll be buying a share and immediately setting a stop loss on that share. The difference between the stock price and the dollar amount the stop loss is set to is the risk of that trade. Targets are always (at least, they should always) calculated in proportion to risk, so in the case of a 1:1 risk to ratio target, the exit point would be the same amount above the stock price as the stop loss was below it.

To clarify: Say you have purchased 1 share of stock XYZ for $50. You set the stop loss at $49.75. This means the risk is $0.25. That's what you stand to lose on this one share if things don't go your way. Therefore, for a scalp, you'll sell the stock when it reaches $50.25.

This means that fundamentally, any trade with a 1:1 ratio is a scalp. But in practice, you'll usually only see the term used in trades with small dollar figures for the risk and potential reward amounts. This is because if they were to be much larger, it would take the market more time to move in either direction before hitting that threshold, and that would remove the risk mitigation benefit that the time limitation provides. Remember our sharks in the pool from before; if they had more time to swim around your hundreds of sponges, you'd be much more likely to lose them.

Identifying the time frames where you can expect upward movement and jumping in, then getting out once your target has been reached is the real key to successful scalping. Because scalping involves multiple mini-trades, often on the same stock, the underlying stock can be evaluated in the same way it would be if it were being assessed for a traditional purchase. Setting targets and sticking with them is a time-honored way to choose your exit point, but there will also be times when it makes more sense to hasten or delay the exit. This is where your day trading instincts and ability to quickly read the market will come into play.

What You'll Need To Be Successful

You'll need to be very comfortable reading the level II quotes in order to scalp successfully. Candlesticks track daily movement, so they are useful in choosing stocks to invest in, but they will not provide the minute-to-minute data that you'll need to time these incredibly short-term trades. You'll also almost certainly need access to a direct-broker to actually place the trades you decide on within the time frames necessary. A live feed and several real-time analysis sources are also invaluable when scalping. Spend some time researching the feeds and analysis providers available in the market you're working in. These are personal decisions because you'll need to be comfortable with them. They'll need to present information in a way that you understand, and that's individual to each trader. The last thing you'll need is a lot of stamina. Making this many split-second decisions is tiring and can get the best of you if you don't have the energy to keep up with them.

Momentum

Momentum trading is sometimes confused with trading on the trend because it does involve buying and selling stocks that are making big moves. Often those moves are in line with the market's direction at the moment. But there are key differences, and those are what make momentum trading suitable for the day trader. Like with trading with the trend, you're going to look for stocks experiencing volatility. The difference is in the amount of volatility. A stock with potential for momentum trades is going to be moving very sharply *and* in high volume. The reasons for this movement determine which type of momentum trade this will be: event-based or technical-based. Even though they function in the same way, it's instructive to look at their differences first.

Event Based Momentum Trades

Arguably more common than technical momentum trades, these occur when a momentum trader chooses a stock that's going to move quickly based on a specific occurrence within the company. Buyouts, new product launches, and restructuring are all examples of events that might create momentum for a stock.

Technical Based Momentum Trades

Technical momentum is movement based on internal factors within the company that are not based on a one-time or rare event. These technical factors are important even when there is an event upcoming, so don't discount them even when you see a juicy-looking launch on the horizon. Instead of an event, technical momentum trades are based solely on the judgement the trader makes on the position of the stock. If, for example, you look at the technicals of a company and determine that is positioned much higher or lower than it should be, and that it will move quickly to correct that, then you've determined that it has technical momentum.

Now that you understand what momentum trades are, let's look at how to find suitable options. Keep in mind that momentum trading can be done with a rising or falling equities using traditional trades or short sales. In the case of short sales, the actions will be opposite to the ones described below, and they'll take place under the same conditions but reversed. So, instead of buying before a stock skyrockets, you'll buy before you expect it to plummet. You'll still exit the trade before a reversal, but instead of selling being your exit strategy, buying will, and the reversal will be in the opposite direction. For purposes of clarity, the explanations below apply to traditional trading.

What To Look For

These are the technical factors all stocks should have in order you to consider them to have momentum, or a potential movement of between 20% and 30% on any given day.

1. Float is the number of shares available to be traded. To find a company's float, subtract the closely-held shares from the number of total shares outstanding. You are looking for a company with a float under about 100 million shares.

2. Daily charts above the moving averages. This means that it will have shown more movement than the average of every other stock's movement.

3. The stock should be free from resistance. If it's close to a resistance pattern, it won't sustain the movement you need to make a momentum trade.

4. Its standard volume numbers should be at least twice the average for the day.

How to Find These Stocks

You'll need to use a stock screener, set with the parameters above in order to narrow your focus to possibly suitable candidates. Then you'll look at equity option calls to see if the stocks that caught your eye have experienced an increase in calls. This indicates that it is likely to move beyond the option premium. This will allow you to create a watchlist of stocks you expect to move much more strongly than the market at large.

Once the trading day begins, you'll track them to see which ones continue to meet your expectations. The ones that do in fact show more movement than the market at large will stay on the list; the rest will be cut.

With these remaining stocks, you'll pull up your level II and the stock's momentum chart and look for indicators of a breakout, meaning sustained periods of momentum that line up with market-maker limit orders piling up and offers starting to slow down. Once you've identified this set of conditions in one of your watch list stocks, that's the one to pick.

How to Execute a Momentum Trade

Once you've found a stock you think will fit all your criteria, you're ready to make your trade. You do not have to immediately place your order, as you will generally not have a problem getting the market price if you're correct about the undervaluation of this equity. This means that you can wait for a tick or two in the movement to confirm, but you absolutely cannot wait too long. Once you have seen the shift you were looking for begin to occur, place your market order.

If you were wrong and the asset's value reverses, sell immediately. It is almost never worth waiting it out. When a volatile stock begins to lose, it usually continues to lose, and badly.

If, however, you were right, now the real fun begins. You have to watch very closely and find the perfect time to jump out of the trade, having made a profit before the movement reverses. This reversal usually happens right after the saturation point is reached, when orders start to slow down, when the level II price starts to slip. You don't have to immediately exit when you see this happen, but it is generally the time to start considering it, and you shouldn't wait too long. You want to be clear before full saturation is in order to ensure you'll be able to find buyers at the price you are hoping to clear. You absolutely never want to keep one of these stocks overnight. The criteria you based your decision to invest on do not hold up during the off-trading hours. Make sure you only buy stock that promises to move quickly so you can avoid this.

Range Trading

Range trading, also called range-bound trading, functions much like normal trading but within the much smaller time frames and movements of the day. In order to do this, you'll need to carefully calculate the support and resistance levels of the security you've chosen and use that information to construct a trendline. The space in between the support and resistance is frequently referred to as the "channel." Unlike momentum trading, if you're range trading you're hoping to avoid those giant movements in price that signal a momentum change. You'll need to look for stocks that show movement only within the channel. This can be risky because if the stock does break out of that channel, it is likely to continue moving in that direction. Take a look at the steps of a range trade to see why that's a problem:

1. Identify the security- This is done just like every other type of day trading. You set out your parameters and then, using stock screeners, data analysis, and your own judgement, select the security that best suits your needs. In the case of range trading, finding a security with a wide enough and strong enough channel to depend upon is key.

2. Buy near the support- Just like traditional trading, the mantra of the range trader is "buy low, sell high." When the price is near its lowest level, according to your calculations, that is your entry point. The opposite is obviously true when buying short, but the principles remain the same.

3. Sell near the resistance- Your calculated upper price limit in the channel is your exit point. This is where you'll place your stop losses (or buy orders in a short.)

As you can imagine, it's a white-knuckle ride during the moments when the price approaches the upper and lower bounds of the channel, and you'll need to have quick reflexes in order to act quickly enough. If the price breaks out of the channel, it's very likely to continue in that direction. This means if it happens, your stop losses are useless to get you out in time. Because of this, you have to watch very closely to make sure that small movements don't become major trends.

Rebate Trading

For scalpers with a lot of capital to invest, rebate trading can be a way to make an extra profit on the side. Some traders do rely solely on rebate trading, but it is rare because the amount of capital required to successfully earn rebates would usually be wasted on such a low-return technique. There are a lot of moving parts in this technique and it's an exceedingly rare technique so we'll explain the principle briefly. If you're interested in this type of trading, the information here will give you enough of a groundwork to build a more detailed rebate trading plan. Even if you don't plan on utilizing this technique it's useful to understand how it works because it sheds some light on the role of market makers and ECNs in the marketplace.

What is Rebate Trading?

Electronic communication networks, which we've mentioned before, are one categorization of broker-dealers. They allow major brokerage firms and traders to work with one another without having to go through an intermediary. They rely on market makers to provide liquidity in the market by filling bids and asks. ECNs reward this behavior by paying rebates to the market makers. Rebate traders trade in ways specifically designed to earn as many of these rebates as possible. This involves a very high number of low-cost trades. The value of the trades themselves frequently doesn't add up to much, making the rebate the majority of the profit involved. When combined with scalping though, the potential for earnings increases greatly.

How To Determine If Rebate Trading Is For You

If you're already scalping successfully at a high volume, it may be worth looking into rebate trading. Especially at first, it's enough for the rebates to simply cover your tax and commission from your other trades. If you're trading on foreign exchanges, ECNs may provide even higher commission rates, so it may be a more attractive option.

Risks and Pitfalls

Rebate trading on its own doesn't earn enough profit for most people to make it worthwhile. If you are just starting out, or if you're not comfortable with another primary strategy, it's best to start somewhere else.

Unless you're trading with a decent sized portfolio, you are unlikely to make enough of a difference in market liquidity for an ECN to consider it worth their while to reward you for it.

The trades that earn these rebates are hundreds, even thousands, of low-value trades. It requires a lot of stamina and a willingness to make a plan and stick to it. If you're not interested in spending every moment glued to your charts, this is probably not the strategy for you, at least at first.

First Hour Trading

The first hour of trading nearly always contains the majority of the movement throughout the day. Day traders placing their orders overnight, money managers and fund managers placing orders for their huge portfolios, responses to overnight news-these all have a dramatic effect on the opening hour or hours of the day. As we've seen, activity equals volatility and that is the stock and trade (so to speak) of the day trader. Many traders find that an hour or two in the morning is all that it takes for them to make enough to cover their taxes and commissions and turn a nice profit.

A Note On Full-Time Trading

Most day traders do not work full time. Whether or not they have another career, for most people it simply doesn't pay to spend eight hours every day at the computer actively trading. For one thing, the stress and intensity can prove overwhelming to even the most seasoned and thick-skinned trader. Another reason is that many traders find they simply don't need to be there. First-hour trading is the most common form this takes, but trading at the open and close, or even just at the close works for a lot of people. As with almost every aspect of day trading, making this decision involves a lot of analysis, looking for relevant patterns, and weighing those realities against your values and goals. Do not skimp on these steps. It can be very tempting to jump into the deep end with both feet, but that's not how careers are made, it's how fortunes are lost.

Finding Entry and Exit Points

We've talked quite a bit about support and resistance levels and now it's time to turn a little more attention to them. Understanding these twin concepts and how they predict market behavior is crucial to knowing when to get in and out of the market. In this chapter, we'll get further into what these forces do and how to spot them.

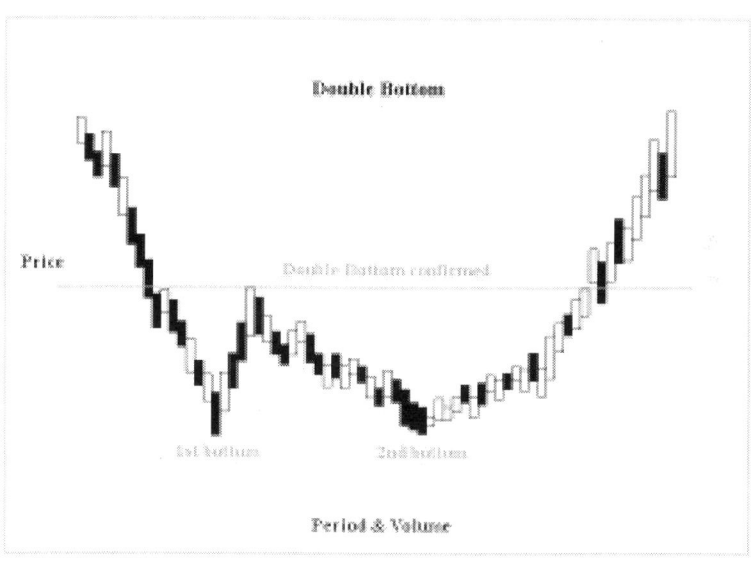

141

The chart above is a good example of support. Look at the two low points, or "bottoms," on the chart. These are points where the price tends to rebound. Once you've calculated a support level, you can expect the price to "bounce" off of it.

Proactive Calculations

Using pivot point calculations, whether your own or from a technical analysis source you trust, is usually the starting point for finding support and resistance levels. Pivot point levels are called "proactive" support or resistance, as opposed to "reactive." What this means is that it is predictive of future behavior, rather than describing current behavior. Remember that no prediction is perfect, and the calculation methods may be proven incorrect. There is a margin of error expected in calculating resistance and support, but if the price continues its motion through the pivot calculation point, that means that a new top or bottom is being found. When this happens, the previous point frequently remains a point of resistance or support, but to a lesser degree. Proactive support and resistance calculations are not set in stone. Rather than reading them as gospel, treat them as guidelines. They'll give you information about where to set your stops, where you should keep a close watch on your assets, and how to calculate your potential reward/risk ratios. Get comfortable with this math because you'll be using it every day.

Reactive Support

An example of reactive support is the candlestick pattern known as "tweezers."

Tweezer Bottoms   **Tweezer Tops**

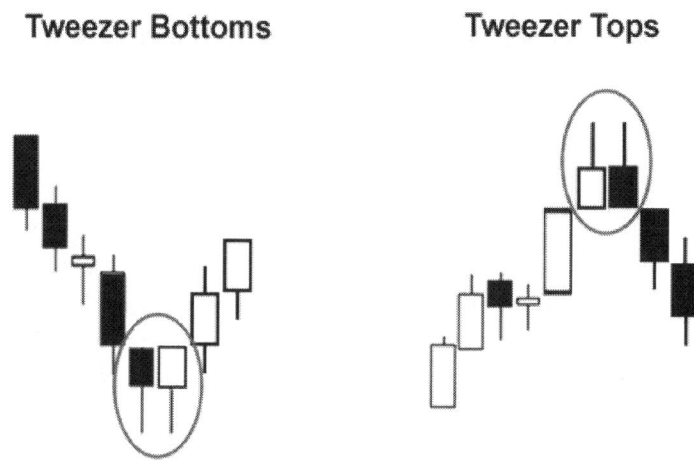

As you can see, they show a reversal in momentum that has already happened. When this stock history shows this pattern repeatedly at a certain price point, this is undoubtedly a marker of resistance or support at that level.

Trendlines

Over time, you may see that support and resistance levels change in a predictable pattern over time. We'll use support as an example, but it works exactly the same way for resistance levels. Let's say that the price of stock XYZ has bounced back up at $80 per share, then $75 per share, then $70 per share. If you were to draw a line through these support levels, you would see that the line trends upward, meaning that support is rising. If your pivot calculation gave you a likely support level at $65 for this stock on this day, you could be very confident in that calculation because it was supported by the trendline. If your pivot calculation was coming to $80 though, you might place slightly less faith in the calculation because it contradicts your trendline.

Round Numbers

An interesting psychological fact about support and resistance levels is how neatly they seem to place themselves at prices ending with "50" and "00." This is entirely due to the fact that people like round numbers and respect them more than other numbers when deciding whether to buy or sell stocks. Practically, this means that if there is a support or resistance at round number, it is much less likely that the price will punch through that level and break out of the prediction.

Futures and Options

Much of this book has so far been concerned with stock trading, and that was intentional as that is what most people trade in. There are other options, however. Futures and options are two other security types that can be utilized by day traders. They do come with their own rewards and challenges, though, so it is highly recommended that you take the time to fully understand these securities before investing in them. Here we will cover some information about them in relation to day trading, but there is much more to learn about them in general.

Futures

One of the biggest advantages to selling futures is the lack of restrictions on short selling. With stocks, many regulators limit short sales in order to stabilize markets occasionally. Futures are exempt from this. Day traders must always be on the lookout for the best transaction available at any given particular time, and those are often short sales. Trading in futures means you'll be able to take advantage of that. Another factor that makes futures day trading attractive is their tendency to gap. It is very common for the opening price to be quite different from the closing price of the day before, meaning gap traders have a lot of room to work. It is common practice for traders to day trade in futures when the market is choppy and volatile and then switch to holding positions for longer periods of time when the markets stabilize and trendlines begin to develop. This allows the trader to take advantage of the high levels of movement when markets are shifting quickly, while letting their traditional positions absorb some risk. It's a fine line though, so this is really only a suitable course if you are well-informed and willing to do the homework required to stay ahead of the market.

Options

Options trading is extremely difficult because not only does the trader have to determine the value of the underlying security, they must also evaluate the option. The price of the option does not necessarily track with the underlying value, so it's hard to know when or if the price will move in a predictable way.

A common mistake beginning options traders make is to buy call options that are out-of-the-money. This seems like a good idea to the novice because it follows the same path as normal stock trading, but it's exceedingly hard to make any money on calls. Remember that unless you're making money, you're losing it to taxes, fees, and commissions.

Another pitfall of options trading is the relative lack of liquidity in the market compared to stocks. The reason behind this is simple: stock traders are all trading the same stock but options traders have more, well, options. There will be multiple options varying by strike price and expiration. This reduces competition and thereby liquidity. This widens the bid-ask spread considerably.

As expirations approach though, liquidity increases. Trading in near-expiration options can be much more profitable than options with expirations many weeks or months away. Put options can also provide protection in a volatile market, so consider them as a replacement or a complement to your options trading.

An easy shorthand for thinking of options trading is that all of the same rules apply but they are turned up to full volume. It's even more important to get out on time, to stick to a plan, and to only make trades that conform to your requirements.

Common Obstacles and How To Avoid Them

1. Taking On Too Much Risk In One Trade

Depending on who you ask, you'll hear that no single trade should take up more than 1%, 2%, 5%, or 10% of your total assets. Which of these is true for you will depend on your risk tolerance. Spoiler: it's probably not 10% unless you are working with a very large amount of money. In almost every case, it is advisable to set your limit low and stick to it. This is going to limit the trades you're able to enter into because your risk/reward ratio won't be met for most trades that come across your desk when you have to stick to these percentages. That's okay! It's actually for the best. Knowing which trades to pick is a key skill, of course, but it's just as important to know which trades not to pick. Being okay with missing an opportunity that might be good for someone but just doesn't suit your needs is a skill that you should begin developing from day one.

2. Pride and the Risk of Doubling Up

One mistake that novices make time and time again is throwing good money after bad. Your emotions might be screaming that a turnaround is right around the corner, but the fact is that when a stock starts dropping, it usually continues to. If a security punches through the support level you calculated, it will most likely keep dropping. There is a natural temptation to buy more stock as the price continues to drop while thinking, "If this was a good deal when I bought it at $2 per share it's an even better deal at $1." While this might be true if you had the time to hold on and wait for a rebound, you're a day trader and you don't have that option. This impulse isn't based on fact or logic, it's based on pride. As hard as it is to admit, you're feeling this need to double down to protect your ability to think of yourself as having been right. The mantra you need for this situation is: The stock market doesn't feel anything about me, I need to not feel anything about it. Your feelings are simply irrelevant. This is why we do the homework, the math, the planning. All of these protect us from relying on emotion.

3. Carrying Overnight

It can be tempting to let a stock run when you feel like it's on a streak, or to give another one time to rebound when you suspect it's going to turn around the next day. Again, this is an emotional decision, not one based on the realities of the market. By this point you will have seen gaps open between closing one day and opening the next; you know well how volatile the market can be even when no active trading is occurring. Do not open yourself up to the risk this entails. In day trading, you need to be able to monitor the movement of the market on a minute-by-minute basis, and you're just not able to stick to your plans and take action when you need to if the market is closed.

4. Skipping Stops

Stop losses serve two purposes: they automate the exit process and prevent you from losing more money than you would without them when things go south and equally importantly, they remove the temptation to let a bad pick dig you into a hole. One thing you will never see an experienced day trader do is skip setting up a stop loss and saying, "I'll just figure it out when I get there." They know that cutting losses quickly and moving on to the next trade is the only way to be successful in the long run. If this book teaches you one thing it should be that this is a numbers game. You don't have to make a mint on every bet. Instead, you just need the totals to add up in your favor over time.

5. Ignoring Risk/Reward Ratios

This is a problem that is very common when traders begin to feel like they are on a "streak." When this happens beginners may be overwhelmed by that feeling and find their thinking clouded. This leads them to invest in bad deals that look attractive at first glance but haven't been properly vetted. Your investing plan should definitely include a risk/reward ratio and times will come when you'll have to remind yourself what it's there for. It's there to prevent you from making bad decisions in the heat of the moment.

6. Over-leveraging or Over-investing

In any investment firm, anywhere in the world, you will hear the following phrase many times throughout the day: Leverage is a double-edged sword. It's a cliche for a reason. Leverage provides hugely increased buying power, but it also gives you the ability to wipe your entire account out in the blink of an eye. Keeping your investments within the percentage of your assets that you determined will help here, but it's also important to keep track of how much leverage you're carrying at any given time. It sounds like a lot of numbers that you're going to have to keep in your head, but there are many software options that will help with this.

Over-investing occurs when beginning traders think that the more they trade, the more they'll earn. The simple fact of the matter is that most days are not going to be days you'll turn any kind of exciting profit. By definition, most days will be fairly average. If you're making dozens of trades a day, chances are it's because you haven't defined the parameters of trades that you'll engage in tightly enough. In fact, once you've been trading for a while, it probably still won't be a good idea to increase your number of daily trades right away. It's often smarter to increase the size of your individual trades instead. After all, what works on 200 shares will work just as well on 400 and it comes with the added benefit of keeping your trading fees the same. If you took that same money and bought 2 different stocks, you'd be doubling your fees.

7. Lack of Focus

Think of this as the dark side of diversification. If you're investing in stocks, foreign markets, options, and futures, you may be thinking that doing this protects you from risk. In reality, though, it's very difficult to gather the expertise it takes to be proficient in all these markets. It's much better to pick a market and a type of security and really get to work studying that asset type. It may happen that as your career progresses you find a different type of investment that catches your interest, but in the beginning, stick to one and become a real expert in it.

8. Slacking on Homework

This is another all-too-common and completely avoidable mistake. Usually what happens is that a trader starts out with the best of intentions, doing their homework and making detailed plans every day. This sets them up for success and they do well, but instead of chalking that up to their hard work they let their pride get in the way. They assume that the reason for their success is their innate ability and not the hours of preparation they've done. They slack off on the homework and then are shocked when they don't do as well. Pride is once again the enemy of the successful trader. Don't let this happen to you! You should have a plan laid out with your overall goals, both long and short term. You should do your homework on every single trade you make. Yes, you will miss out on some trades that end up making someone money but that's fine. You'll also keep yourself out of trades that don't work out and could potentially cost you everything. Meticulous research and planning is the only way to be successful in the long term.

If you've made it this far, you are well on your way to entering the market and becoming a successful day trader. Keep in mind that this is only the beginning and there is much more to learn as your career progresses. As you find different types of assets to invest in, you'll specialize and build skills in those particular areas. This is what will set you apart from other day traders and give you an edge as you move forward in those markets. Make sure you keep learning, keep a cool head, and keep meticulous records and you'll be well on your way to a lucrative and exciting day trading career.

DAY TRADING:

Tips and Tricks to Start Right, Avoid Mistake and Win with Day Trading

By Samuel Rees

Introduction

Congratulations on downloading *Day Trading: Tips and Tricks to Start Right, Avoid Mistake and Win with Day Trading* and thank you for doing so. While the right types of individuals with the right types of systems can certainly profit from day trading, that doesn't mean that this type of market interaction is for everyone. While the only way to truly know if this type of short term trading is right for you is to see it in action, the following tips and tricks will certainly be useful in at least pointing you in the right direction when that day comes.

To that end, the following chapters will discuss everything you need to get started in day trading successfully including how to make the type of personalized trading plan that will ensure you are successful more often than not. You will also learn many of the tips for success that even the most veteran day traders use on the regular so that you can emulate them moving forward. This is followed by numerous mistakes that new day traders make along with the easiest ways to ensure you don't share the same fate. You will then learn several important day trading strategies including how to effectively use technical analysis, how to take advantage of first hour trading and how to find a profit trading momentum.

There are plenty of books on this subject on the market, thanks again for choosing this one! Every effort was made to ensure it is full of as much useful information as possible,

please enjoy! It is important to always take any type of
investment very seriously and to always understand that no
matter how much of a sure thing a given investment appears
to be it can still fail to meet expectations. As such, it is
recommended that you never invest more than you can afford
to lose.

Chapter 1:

Make a Personalized Trading Plan

If you are interested in ensuring that you do more than simply avoid losing your shirt when you start day trading on the regular, then the first thing you are going to need to do is create the type of personalized trading plan that ensures it is more likely to make a profit than not when used in the wild. It isn't enough just to create the plan, however, you are also going to need to have the dedication and mental determination to stick with it, even when your emotions are in overdrive, which is a skill that can only reliably be counted on with practice.

Consider your strengths and weaknesses: In order to ensure that the plan that you end up with is one that you will actually be able to make use of, the first thing you are going to need to do is to consider your level of experience with the stock market in the past and how successful you have been at trading previously. The fast paced nature of day trading means that it is going to take more innate knowledge and skill than some of the other investment markets that you could start off in. As such, it is important that when it comes to creating a plan that works for you, you also consider various other weaknesses that may hinder you when it comes to day trading and also those skills that will be able to give you an edge over the competition.

During this personal evaluation you are going to want to be certain that you take a look at yourself through an analytical lens as overestimating your abilities will do nothing except set you up for bigger losses, sooner than later. This analysis isn't a test, there are no winners or losers, the goal is to get as accurate view of the whole picture as possible, nothing more. Of special import is how likely you believe it to be that you will ignore your plan in the heat of the moment when all of your emotions are running hot. If you can control yourself then great, otherwise you will likely find it helpful to put additional safeguards in place, to save yourself from yourself.

Take into account other challenges you might face: When it comes to building your own plan, you will want to be sure to keep in mind any external challenges you might have to deal with in addition to the internal ones. Challenges in this vein are typically things like lacking the ideal resources for a perfect start or personal issues that makes planning for the future more difficult than it otherwise might be. The point is that you are going to want to be well aware of what you are fighting against in addition to the traditional inconsistencies in the market. Failing to take these types of challenges into account up front is always going to lead to a decreased overall success rate.

Decide how much risk is acceptable: The amount of risk that is right for you is going to be different than the amount of risk that is right for anyone else which is why it is so important to create your own plan instead of simply copying someone else's. To determine the amount of risk that is right for you, you are going to want to start by determining what the total amount that you have available to work with is going to be. As a rule of thumb you should never commit more than 5 percent of the total you have to work with into any single trade as this is a good way to ensure you don't ever put more into a trade than you can afford to lose. Additionally, many day traders prefer to only take on trades that they believe are going to pay out 300 times what they cost to buy into to ensure they are being adequately compensated for their time.

These two numbers are what makes up what is known as a risk/reward ratio and it can be easily determined by simply taking how much you realistically expect to make on a trade and then dividing that number by the amount you have to put down on the trade. You goal should be results that are higher than 3 if you are going to go ahead and pull the trigger. This won't tell you how likely the trade is going to end in success, however, which is why it is important to understand what your tolerance for risk is before moving forward.

To determine your level of tolerance to risk, the first thing you are going to want to do is to consider how much time you are going to spend playing the market and what types of returns you need to see in order to make the experience worth your time. The less time you have to spend trading, the more risk you are going to need to be able to accept in order to generate the same amount of return. If you don't like the results, you can either change the amount of time you are willing to commit to the endeavor or the amount you are expecting to get back, there aren't any other options.

Choose the right exit and entry points: When it comes to ensuring that you meet your goals, it is important to always go into a given trade with a clear idea of the point that you will either be happy with your profits and walk away or be unwilling to take a greater loss and do the same. While many less experienced traders will always feel the need to stay in after the signs clearly point that the time to exit has past either to squeeze a little extra from the trade they are currently dealing with, the truth of the matter is that this is going to lead to a greater overall loss in the long term, guaranteed. The exit points that you choose should be dictated by your level of risk tolerance and should never be changed in the midst of a trade when your emotions are likely going to be at their peak.

When it comes to choosing an entry point that is likely to be profitable, you are going to want to lean into your level of acceptable risk and to choose trades that meet the parameters that you feel comfortable with. It is important to always be true to yourself in this instance as working against your natural inclinations will only lead to trouble in the long run.

Chapter 2:

Tips for Success

It's still all about supply and demand: While there are a lot of complicated theories and strategies that go along with day trading, the root of the entire market runs on supply and demand, just like any other market does, which means that if you look for periods where supply and demand are unbalanced you can use them to your advantage when it comes to choosing the most effective entry points possible. When supply is low then prices are naturally going to be higher which means that it is time to sell and if there is a lull in demand then you are going to want to buy to take advantage of that. You will still want to learn everything there is to know about the market, just don't forget the basics when all is said and done.

Implement daily limits: While knowing how much risk you can successfully deal with in a given trade is key to making progress as a day trader, you will still find yourself unable to make a profit if you don't limit how much you can lose in a day before you stop trading in order to prevent yourself from mentally getting in your own way and making your losses much worse as a result. A good rule of thumb is that if you find yourself down a full 10 percent of your total investment amount you should stop for the day to give yourself the time you need to recover. As long as you know your plan is effective

60 percent of the time or more then you don't need to worry about tweaking, all you need to do is wait for the market to be in a better mood.

Keep a trading journal: While you should never set weekly or daily profit goals as this will only promote bad trading habits as you start to make unreasonably risky trades in order to meet, or attempt to meet, these goals, you will want to keep track of all of your trades, profitable and unprofitable so that you can get an overall idea of how your plan is working out and how you are progressing. You will want to make note of the stocks that you traded, the date, the time, the reason you decided to make the trade, the movement after the fact and how much you made, or lost in the bargain. While looking at these things daily or weekly won't give you the data that you need to make a real estimation one way or the other, checking into your results once a month is encourage to ensure you aren't following a plan that was successful for a time only to have dropped off since.

Never become personally invested in the stocks: It is easy for new traders to become personally invested in specific trades that they have made which makes losses in those cases much more difficult to handle than they might otherwise be. It is important to always remain analytical about the trades you are currently considering and never do anything if you feel as though you wouldn't have done the same at the beginning of the trading period when you were at your best. Specifically, you are going to want to avoid making the mistake of doubling down on a stock that has served you well in the past but has since been headed down with no remorse in an effort to hypothetically profit from its return to glory should it occur.

This is little more than throwing good money after bad, however, and should be avoided whenever possible.

Be as robotic as possible: When it comes to day trading successfully it is important to make it a point to make the act of finding which stocks to trade as machine like and rout as possible. You want your day to involve little more than finding stocks that match your plan, buying into those stocks until they hit your stops, rinse and repeat. The only thought you should have is whether or not a given stock meets the requirements of your plan and how many shares you should by. Avoid looking for thrills and you will see a greater overall return on your initial investment in the long term.

Understand the current mood of the market: All of the technical analysis (discussed in chapter 5) will only take you so far when it comes to trading successfully as you will just as often find yourself dealing with the will of the market as a whole as you will with the specifics related to a given stock. This means you are going to need to worry about what the other traders around you are thinking as much as you need to be aware of what it is the market is actually doing. As long as you make it a point to know what the general temperature of the market is, as well as what any major players you are watching are up to, then you accurately plan your moves and profit from those who aren't smart enough to do the same.

Wait for the right trade: Many new traders find themselves feeling as though the times they aren't actively working a trade are wasted and try and fix this problem by making as many trades in a given day as possible. It is easy to overtrade in this mentality, however, and lose out on any of the profit that previous good decisions may have brought you. While it may initially seem as though you are missing out, the truth of the matter is that quality over quantity will almost always serve you better than the other way around. Anywhere between 3 and 5 quality trades a day can be enough to find long lasting success as long as you know how to work those trades properly.

Take the right message from failed trades: Even the best traders on the planet don't reach 100 percent trade success, at least not regularly, which means that hoping every one of your trades is going to be successful is nice, it is far from realistic. Instead, it is important to focus on properly executing on every trade so that even if it ultimately doesn't work out as you have hoped, you can still take comfort in the fact that you did everything right on your end.

Chapter 3:

Mistakes to Avoid

*C*hoosing the wrong broker: As their minds are typically focused on other things, many new day traders make the mistake of choosing the first broker that they find without taking the time to research anything about them. If you are having problems with your broker then it is too late to start doing research, you are going to be putting your investment capital in their hands so you should make sure you know where those hands have been. The truth of the matter is that it doesn't take much to create a website that appears to be on the level and new websites clamming to be brokers, and filled with malicious intent, pop up every single day.

Even if the broker that you do choose to do business with really is on the level, it is important to dig into their customer service history to determine not just that they provide adequate customer service, but also that their technology is completely up to date and as fast as it can be, remember, in day trading every millisecond counts. This means that if you see complaints of orders not getting to the exchange with a quickness, you will want to look elsewhere as this is a service that can definitely be provided by a truly competent broker.

Not having up to date technology: Day trading is a game of inches and the changes that can happen in the blink of an eye can be enough to make or break the success streak that you have been courting all day long. Remember, even if you think the technology that you are using to trade is good enough, you aren't just trading against the market, you are trading against other traders, both big and small, who are all trying to one up one another with the best technology on the market today. While this doesn't mean that you need to go out and buy a $3,000 computer, it does mean that you will want to have a rig that can compete with the current generation of hardware if you hope to make the sorts of split second trades that ultimately lead to major windfalls in the long run.

Even with the best technology, however, it is important that you always enter into every trade with stop losses clearly posted in case for whatever reason you cannot pull the trigger on the second part of a given trade in a timely fashion. You will also want to ensure that you have a landline so that even if your internet goes down and magically takes your cell phone with it you will still be able to contact your broker and complete the trade in question. While this might seem like overkill, it won't after you fail to close a six figure trade because of a freak occurrence. An ounce of prevention is worth a pound of cure and in this case the pound is solid gold.

Getting in at the wrong time: As a new day trader it can be difficult to get your bearings which means that when you do happen upon a specific trend it can be easy to jump on it now and ask questions about it later. While this might lead to success from time to time, the fact of the matter is that spotting a trend at the right time is much more important than spotting it in the first place. The most profitable time to spot a trend is right as it is beginning as this way you will have the most possible time to turn a profit as it matures. When it comes to finding trends early, it will help to have an idea of who the major players are in the types of stocks that you tend to favor. Major players are anyone whose movement alone is enough to alter the state of the market and getting to know them, and watching them like a hawk, is key to your long term success as a day trader.

Not balancing research with the current truth: New day traders typically fall into two camps, those who do too much research before starting out and those that don't do enough research before starting out. Those that do too much research tend to consider every aspect of the companies that they are thinking about purchasing stock in and only purchase when the fundamentals appear to be completely on the up and up. Unfortunately, they then tend to stick with their analysis, even when the reality of the market says that public sentiment has turned on the stock in question which means that it is going to tank and not see the light of day for a good long while. Doing research is key, but so is looking at the facts as they currently stand and making informed decisions based on what you see.

On the other hand, are the new traders who only think about what the market currently has to say about a stock in question. While this will often lead them to making the right decision in the moment, it will then be difficult for them to determine the next step as they won't be able to tell if the current price is over or undervalued based on the history or the fundamentals of the underlying company. Only by taking both into account, and updating that account every single day can you ever truly hope to find success as a day trader.

Not treating day trading like a job: If you ever hope to day trade full time, the first thing you are going to need to do is to treat trading as though it were already a job. What this means is committing to it for the same period of time every day, no

matter what. If day trading is a job, then this means you are
going to have to be your own boss which means you will need
to keep tabs on your comings and goings and ensure you
dedicate the time you need to trading each day in order to
reach your goals. While staring at a bunch of numbers on a
screen can make it easy to feel disconnected from what is
actually happening, it will only take one trip to the bathroom
with trades on the table to teach you how real what you are
doing actually is.

Chapter 4:

Using Technical Analysis

When it comes to ensuring that your successful trade percentage only increases as time goes on, you may find it useful to branch out of analyzing the fundamentals of a company to determine if its stock is worth considering and to also analyze it technically. Technical analysis studies past market trends with the goal of accurately predicting those that are likely to occur again in the future. Technical analysis is ideal for those that like the idea of determining future performance by looking at previous prices, without having to dig through mountains of paperwork to find the details you are looking for. While the past will never be able to truly predict the future 100 percent of the time, technical analysis is useful when combined with a basic understanding of market mentality for generating predictions that are accurate within reason.

Price charts: A price chart is a core part of technical analysis; essentially, it is a chart with both an x and a y axis where the price can be seen along the vertical axis and the time can be seen along the horizontal axis. While there are plenty of different charts to choose from, each with their own unique strengths and weaknesses, those that you will want to keep in mind early on include the line chart, the candlestick chart, the bar chart and the point and click chart.

Line chart: The line chart is the simplest of all the charts
because all it does is show the closing price of a given stock
over a set period of time. The lines, in this case, are formed
once the grouping of closing prices has been determined and
then connected with the end goal of showing a trend. You
won't be able to find details such as what the opening price for
the same period of time was or what the overall results for the
day were but you will be able to determine if the day over day
is positive which is still quite important which is why this is
one of the first charts that day traders of all skill levels consult
when they are looking into the details of a new stock.

Bar chart: A bar chart expounds upon the details provided by
a line chart by providing a greater degree of detail regarding
the specifics of the day. The top and bottom of the bar
represent the high and the low for the day respectively while
the price at closing is indicated on the ride side of the bar with
the help of a handy dash. The dash on the left side of the bar
shows the starting price. and if the stock increased in value for
the day then the bar will be black while it will either be red or
clear if the price decreased throughout the day.

Candlestick chart: A candlestick chart is similar to a bar chart,
though the information it provides is much more detailed
overall. Like a bar chart it includes a line to indicate the range
for the day, however, when you are looking at a candlestick
chart you will notice a wide bar near the vertical line which
indicates the degree of difference the price saw throughout the
day. If the price that the stock is trading at increases overall
for the day, then the candlestick will often be clear while if the
price has decreased then the candlestick is going to be read.

Point and figure chart: While seen less frequently than some
of the other types of charts, a point and figure chart has been

around for nearly a century and can still be useful in certain situations today. This chart can accurately reflect the way price is going to move, though it won't indicate timing or volume. It can be thought of as a pure indicator of price with the excessive noise surrounding the market muted, ensuring nothing is skewed.

A point and figure chart is noticeable because it is made up of Xs and Os rather than lines and points. The Xs will indicate points where positive trends occurred while the Os will indicate periods of downward movement. You will also notice numbers and letters listed along the bottom of the chart which correspond to months as well as dates. This type of chart will also make it clear how much the price is going to have to move in order for an X to become an O or an O to become an X.

Trend or range: When it comes to using technical analysis successfully, you will want to determine early on if you are more interested in trading based on the trends you find or on the range. While they are both properties related to price, these two concepts are very different in practice which means you will want to choose one to emphasize over the other. If you decide to trade according to trend, then you are more interested in going with the flow and choosing stocks to trade while everyone else is having the same idea.

Your goal in this instance is to then determine what trends are going to manifesting themselves in the future so that you have as much time to take full advantage of them as possible. If you are interested in trying this type of trading you will want to make smaller than average trades as it can be risky as you never know when a trend will fail to materialize in the way you might have previously hope it would. Trading via trend is a good choice for those who prefer high risk and high reward trades.

If you are interested in a safer trading strategy, then you will want to consider range trading instead. When you are trading on the range, you are instead looking for stocks that you can reliably predict with relative confidence will make a positive movement before moving back to about where they started from before repeating the cycle once more. You don't need to find the perfect entry point in this instance, you simply need to get in at a point where you will be in on the ground floor the next time the cycle repeats itself. Range trading can take more time to get working properly, however, so it is best to have a larger bankroll when aiming to successfully put it into effect.

Chapter 5:

First Hour Trading

The truth of the matter is that, while the market is open all day long, the majority of the trading that occurs will do so either during the first hour of the day or the last. As such, new day traders can make things a lot easier on themselves by starting off exclusively focusing on the first hour of trading. When done correctly, sticking to first hour trading will allow to generate enough liquidity to get in and get out as soon as the market solidifies for the day. Studies show that the market only continues to trend roughly 20 percent of the time which means that most of the time the market won't be doing much of anything. This type of strategy does require a good deal of volume in order to be successful, which means that it is best undertaken by those who have at least $100,000 worth of investment capital available to start with.

First hour breakdown

Opening 5 minutes: The 5-minute chart is by far the most common chart that day traders refer to and this starts from the first 5 minutes. This is enough time to start seeing volume and price of various stocks start to spike as gaps start to form based on the differences between yesterday's close and today's open. You will often be able to get a general idea of what is

going on in this arena from news or announcements that break
or are rumored to break in the early morning hours.

The rules and parameters for the day have not yet codified,
however, so this period of time is also one of the most volatile
of the entire day. The gap from the previous day makes
establishing a range impossible which, in turn, makes trading
during this period akin to little more than gambling and there
are certainly easier ways to gamble than via day trading. All
told, you will want to be aware of what the market is doing in
this time frame but avoid interacting with it yourself if you
don't like the idea of gambling with your money.

Between 9:30 and 9:50: While this segment might seem a
little non-traditional, the fact of the matter is that there are
numerous reasons to jump in prior to the 10 am segment and
the first of which is the relative lack of competition. By making
a move at before the hour you will get the jump on those who
are waiting for the full 30-minute chart as well as the latest 15-
minute chart, while at the same time only increasing your risk
a modest amount as things have typically started to settle
down at this point.

This is the time you will then want to determine what the low
and high values for the morning actually are as this will help
you determine the types of clearly defined price points that
indicate boundaries on the stock you are considering. If the
stock in question then moves past the points you have
established then you can safely assume that they are showing
the beginnings of a trend. Once these trends have been
established you will then be able to determine if it is going to
be more profitable for you to trade with the trend or against it.

Between 9:50 and 10:10: This is the time period where you are going to want to make a bigger move based on the results from the first 20-minute period. This is the period of time when you are going to want to enter all of your trades for the day if you are trading the first hour as if you wait until 10:15 am, or later, then you will be severely hampering your ability to make a profit even if you make all the right decisions up until this point.

Between 10:10 and 10:30: During the final 20 minutes of the cycle, you are going to want to let the stock smoothly follow the trends that you noticed early on. While this might not seem like much, the reality is that if you got in at 9:50 am, then 10:30 am is 40 minutes which can make for a lot of time for movement during the early part of the day. You will be able to realistically wait until as late as 11:00 am if things are really moving well, though at the first sign of slowdown you are typically better off getting out. It is important to never just let your morning trades run on cruise control as you never know when things might switch directions, destroying your profits in the process. Remember, the odds that things will continue moving in your favor enough to make a real difference once things have slowed for the day are much lower than the state of the market changing and costing you money instead.

During the last 20 minutes you are going to want to be paying close attention to the signs that it is time to get while the getting is good. It is important to know what you exit goal is before you get started to ensure that you aren't too busy worrying about working out the details that you actually miss the signals you were looking for.

Instead of being worried about missing out on every single dollar that you could possibly earn on a trade, it is much more productive to worry about losing out on existing profits instead. Make a point of setting profit targets for all of your trades and then once you hit them, get out when the getting is good. Over time, you will find that if you guard your existing profits, rather than pinning over the profits that might have been, your results will be much more reliable. If you hit your target, but the movement on the underlying stock is still so prominent that you hate to miss out on what could be a significant additional windfall, the right choice may instead be to split the difference.

Specifically, you would then want to sell off half of your shares before setting a new stop loss at the current price so that you will be able to cash out the other half for a profit no matter what. You will then want to set a new price target for the remaining shares and repeat the process as needed. While you may not make as much as you ultimately would have if you had kept all of your shares, at the same time you prevent yourself from losing out on all the profit you have already made which is more important in the long run.

Chapter 6:

Day Trading Based on Momentum

Whether it comes to making a profit in the short term, putting momentum to work for you is one of the best ways of doing so regardless of what your overall skill level with day trading happens to be. The goal of the momentum breakout strategy is to catch stocks while they are in a period of heavy momentum and take advantage of that fact. This means you are going to be able to keep track of which stocks are moving and to which degree, something that can easily be done with any stock scanning software.

Momentum is the rate at which a stock accelerates either in the speed or the force of its movement. Momentum can also be thought of as the price movement's rate of change or the speed at which that price is changing. When using this type of strategy, you are going to want to take a long position on a stock that is trending positively and a short position on stock that is trending negatively. When it comes to momentum investing your goal should be to sell low and then buy in even lower or buy high and then sell at a point that is higher still. Momentum trading is unconcerned with patterns of reversal or continuation and instead focus simply on the trend that was created after the most recent price break.

As a day trader who is focused on momentum, you are going to be primarily interested in performance, which means choosing stocks that are further in both extremes in hopes of achieving what are known as alpha returns with stocks that are trending in a particular direction. If a stock has positive momentum, then it is considered hot and if it has negative momentum it is said to be cold.

Momentum trading breakdown

Start with the research: When it comes to momentum trading, the first thing that you are going to want to do each morning is get a feel for the state of the market as it stands. This means that an hour or so before the market opens you are going to want to visit the most popular subreddits and other message boards related to day trading that you favor to determine which stocks are being talked about the most.

This means you will want to take note of stocks that are being talked about in trading alerts thanks to their earnings or other recommendations. These are the stocks that are considered to be the most relevant for your purposes today which means you will want to dig a bit deeper and determine which, have had the greatest increase in calls. This will give you an idea of which prices are likely to vary the most dramatically as soon as the market opens.

Market Open: After the market opens you will want to pay special attention the stocks that you have already earmarked for further consideration to see how they move in relation to the market as a whole. It is important to be aware if they are increasing at a greater rate than the market as a whole and if they are behaving the way you expected them to in your initial assessment. You will use this period of time to further hone in on the stocks that appear to be the most promising, ideally with a rapidly increasing price and a high volume when compared to the market as a whole. These are the stocks that are clearly being influenced by external factors which means they are not bound by the traditional rules.

Look to the charts: With the final list of stocks for the day in mind, the next thing you are going to want to do is look at the charts for each of the stocks separately. The technical indicator that you are looking for in this case is going to be momentum, in this case indicated by the amount of net change between the closing price over a prolonged period of time. This line will then be plotted against the price chart to determine either prolonged positive or negative movement. This exercise will often point to periods of breakout, which you will want to move in front of to ensure that you are able to take full advantage of the prolonged upward or downward movement. It doesn't matter if you miss the earliest moments of a breakout, as long as you manage to get in on the action before it truly begins in earnest.

Enter a trade and wait: Once you have found the breakout that you are looking for to indicate the best time to enter the market, you are going to want to make the type of trade that it indicates and then get ready to wait. The amount of momentum that a breakout will be able to sustain will be difficult to determine accurately before you go ahead and make your move so the period after you do so will be a waiting game where you wait to see when the momentum in question starts to fade.

If you find that the momentum you were following dissipates almost immediately, it is important to cut your losses as quickly as possible and get out of the trade rather than trying to ride out the reversal in hopes of things returning to the course you've charted. Once the momentum you were riding dissipates, there is no guarantee it is ever coming back which means that the only thing you can do in these instances is cut your losses and start from scratch. If you are going to use this strategy you will need to ensure your emotions never get in the way of letting you pull the trigger to cut a bad trade loose.

When it comes to investing successfully using this strategy it is important to always take timing into account, both when it comes to jumping off of a trade gone wrong and also when it comes to jumping in at the start. It can be easy to want to jump the gun and commit to a stock after it shows the first signs of gaining momentum, this is a fool's errand, however, as without doing all of the required research you are essentially just guessing which is of no good to anyone.

Conclusion

Thank you for making it through to the end of *Day Trading: Tips and Tricks to Start Right, Avoid Mistake and Win with Day Trading*, let's hope it was informative and able to provide you with all of the tools you need to achieve your goals whatever it is that they may be. Just because you've finished this book doesn't mean there is nothing left to learn on the topic, expanding your horizons is the only way to find the mastery you seek.

When it comes to going from a novice day trader to an expert and master of the market, it is important to approach the task with the appropriate mindset for true success. This means that you will need to anticipate that it will take some time for everything to properly click into place and that it is perfectly normal to have a rocky few weeks when you find your trade footing. As long as you perfect the trading plan for you and keep at it, however, eventually things should right themselves and you should see your profits start to move in the opposite direction.

Regardless of what steps you take, and how carefully you go about mitigating all the risk that you run across, it is also important to understand that there is some risk you will never be able to get rid of completely, nor would you want to. While sometimes this risk means that an otherwise surefire trade isn't going to work out the way you planned, if there was no risk then there could be no reward as prices would always proceed as planned and profits would remain uniform and uninspired. Instead of shying away from risk at all its levels, it is best that you embrace it for what it is, a tool that can be brought to the forefront as needed with clear expectations as to what use it will be and what results it will produce overall.

Finally, if you found this book useful in anyway, a review on Amazon is always appreciated!

DAY TRADING:

The Advanced Guide that Will Make You the KING of Day Traders

By Samuel Rees

Introduction

Congratulations on downloading *Day Trading: The Advanced Guide that Will Make You the KING of Day Traders* and thank you for doing so. This book will take you beyond the information you may have learned in my beginner's guide to day trading. Hopefully by this point, you have either taken some of the advice from the beginner's guide and have been researching diligently the topic of day trading, or maybe you have even started to actually make trades on the stock market. Either way, this book will address topics that you may still be unsure of or about which you have questions. It's a simple fact that while you may already be earning money on the stock market through day trading, there are always going to be techniques that you can learn and areas of your skillset upon which you can improve. For any trader, one of the most important aspects of developing successful strategies is to always keep educating yourself. You have taken this crucial step by downloading this book. Congratulations!

The following chapters will discuss many advanced aspects of day trading, such as mistakes that you might be making and how you can avoid them and advanced strategies that are often too complex for the beginner day trader to grasp. The two types of strategies on which we'll be focusing are the contrarian philosophy to investing and the momentum philosophy to investing. After you're finished reading this book, there's no doubt in my mind that you'll be well on your way to seeing even higher profits than you already are. If you haven't yet started to day trade, don't panic. This book has been compiled in a comprehensive way, so that you don't have to waste time shuffling through information that may or may not be useful to you at a later date. Trust me, while this information may not be useful now, it will certainly be useful in the future at one point or another. In this way, you should be able to use this book as your guide throughout your entire day trading journey. You'll be able to look back on it and reference it as certain scenarios arise in real time. It doesn't get much better than that, and many books that talk about the stock market cannot offer you such a concise piece of work.

There are plenty of books on this subject on the market, thanks again for choosing this one! Every effort was made to ensure it is full of as much useful information as possible, please enjoy!

Chapter 1:

Ten Common Day Trader Mistakes That You Might Be Making without Knowing It

I f you have already started to day trade, but feel generally unfulfilled day after day due to your struggles with the market and an inability to make money, you're not alone. There are many day traders out there who quickly become frustrated and end up quitting on this potentially lucrative field before they can realize their full potential. This chapter will try to rectify some of the mistakes that you might be making without even knowing it. In comparison to other types of trading that is available to you, day trading is one of the more difficult fields to get used to. Of course, once you get the hang of it, making money can seem almost too easy at time, but it can also take time to get to a place where profits are more common than debt. This chapter will look at the mistakes that many day traders make on a constant basis, even the good ones. Remember as we go through this chapter that you're never alone in the sense that there is always room for improvement. All day traders (and truthfully all stock investors in general) get better with experience. Recognizing these mistakes will help you to make better investments in both the short and long term.

Day Trading Mistake 1: You Trade Too Often

If you are one of those people who imagine yourself becoming a guru of trading in a few short weeks, you have some reevaluating to do. We would all love to be investors such as those from the movie the "Wolf of Wall Street", but these types of movies simply do not depict reality. When you're trading your stocks, you should be focusing on those shares that show a high probability for success. Operating from the perspective that there is an equal chance that many deals will work out for you is just the wrong way to do it. I know good and successful day traders who only end up trading one or two stocks a day. They're diligent in their research and legwork and they certainly know what they're doing, but this is usually the boring reality of day trading. There's not always going to be days when you're trading ten stocks an hour, although of course there will be some days when you are trading more frequently than others.

Additionally, sometimes the thinking is that if you are finding success through the current volume in which you're trading stock that you should start to trade this same amount of stock with more frequency. This is absolutely the wrong approach to take. Instead of increasing the frequency in which you trade stock, you should consider instead trading stock in higher volumes. For example, if you have been getting used to trading two hundred shares of a certain stock and are seeing an average positive return on this money, you should consider doubling it to four hundred shares, or increase it by any type of margin. When you change the volume instead of the frequency in which you're trading, it's more likely that you're going to see the same success that you have been seeing previously. The simple fact of the matter is that if you change something that's already working, you run the risk of ruining an already good thing.

Day Trading Mistake 2: Forgetting to Develop a Business Plan

In my first book on the topic of day trading, we talked a lot about how it's important to forgo any emotional attachments that you may have to your investments. It's hard for some day traders to remember that at the end of the day, stock trading is business and not a hobby or a willy-nilly endeavor. The general thinking is this: if you don't write down your strategies and business plan goals for day trading in a comprehensive manner, you're more than likely going to be giving your money away to someone who does have a serious plan and they're following it like clockwork.

If you've ever written a business plan for a small business, then you already are one step ahead of the game. In general, a business plan will document your objectives for day trading, your general plan including how much money you plan on spending, and how you will go about conducting your trades. Other factors that should also be inside of your business plan include what shares you will trade, which markets you will trade on, your entry and exit strategies, and any specific contracts that you plan on using. If you don't have a formal, written-out business plan in place already, you run the risk of engaging in deals through the passion that you feel towards a particular trade, rather than using rational logic to accomplish your goals and win money. Additionally, some of the best business plans for day trading also often answers to various scenarios instead of a single situation. If you can think ahead of time about how you are going to deal with a certain situation, you'll be able to recall this information quickly when you're trading. This will also help to counter emotional trading that may arise when you're first starting out. Lastly, don't feel like you can't go back and alter your business plan over time. This should be a working document. The longer that you day trade, the more experience you're going to accrue. Over time, you'll have more scenarios that you can enter into your business plan. If you keep updating your business plan, not only will you have a great resource for yourself. You'll also be able to see how and where you've evolved as a day trader.

Day Trader Mistake 3: Having Unrealistic Expectations

Often times, day traders who are both new to the industry and even those who have be trading for quite some time forget that hard work is essential in the stock trading world. This myth is what causes many day traders to waste large amounts of time searching for that secret formula for easy trading that does not exist. Instead of trying to figure out the secret sauce of trading, a better idea is to simply come to the table well-prepared. Polish your own strategies, and keep adequate documentation on all of the actions that you're making. This way, you'll be able to see what is working and what isn't working for you, and you'll be able to tweak your strategy until you find success. Remember, it's extremely unlikely that you're going to make one million dollars easily through the stock market. Day trading in particular requires plenty of patience, attention to detail, and the ability to admit to yourself when you're wrong. That last quality is easier for some and harder for others to come to terms with.

Day Trader Mistake 4: Failing to be Disciplined Enough

There's a chance that while you consider yourself to be fairly disciplined, nothing could be further from the truth. For example, in my advanced book on stock trading I discussed how stop-loss orders are essential and must be used when trading shares. Stop-loss orders are commonly known as "damage control" mechanisms because they limit the amount of money that you can lose. If you don't have the wherewithal or the discipline to use these types of strategies when you need to, you're going to miss out on the opportunities that are staring you in the face. Remember, the opportunities are going to always exist on the stock market. It's how you approach these opportunities that ultimately determines whether you win or lose.

Discipline is often nothing more than damage control. It's important to also think about whether or not you're naturally a disciplined person. You can look to other areas of your life to figure this out. For example, are your areas of living usually messy or clean? Do you find your office space to be cluttered or pristinely organized? If you are asking yourself these questions only to find that you are not as disciplined as you may have thought, it will be a good idea to structure your business plan and overarching day trading strategies in a way that will ensure that you have to be disciplined. Discipline, by definition, involves the execution of small tasks over and over. While this type of activity may seem boring, it's typically the smaller tasks that can set you up for a large success.

Day Trading Mistake 5: Altering Your Strategy Too Often

It's most likely that you already know this by now, but day trading is not a type of trading in which gains are always coming your way. It's not unheard of for a day trader to experience loss after loss after loss, and only to experience a gain in a small increment once in a while. It is common for investors to think that if their strategy doesn't bring them success within 5 trades, then their strategy must be a poor one. You may not be aware of this, but it's a proven fact that it can take up to ten losing trades in a row before you end up with a win. Day trading requires a particular type of patience, and if you are constantly changing your strategy, then you're not going to ever realize what ultimately works for you strategically. Additionally, a potentially unfortunate but nonetheless actual reality of day trading is that mistakes are crucial to your overall path to success. As with most things in life, if you don't make mistakes, you're never going to figure out how to navigate the market as a whole. Be patient, give your strategy time to work itself out on the trading floor, and you will most likely see your losing streak turn into a winning one.

Day Trading Mistake 6: You Don't Conduct Post-Trading Analysis

Maybe you've already heard of a post-trading analysis, but there's also a chance that you haven't. A post-trading analysis can be best defined as a summary of how your previous trades have either failed or been successful, with markers that point to all of the basics that you learned about in current events. Yes, that's right, the five W's that are who, what, when, where and why should all be included in your post-trading analysis. Let's go through each one quickly.

Who: Obviously, you are the one making your own trades (unless you have made some sort of negotiation with a brokerage service, in which case that is an exception to this scenario); however, if you find that when you ask yourself about the "who" of your transaction that you are pointing to others who have told you to do something with your own shares, then you know that you have some reevaluating to do. For example, if you find yourself thinking to yourself something along the lines of, "Well...of course I made this trade but it was really Lucy who advised me to do it this way..." then there's a chance that you have some changes to make. Of course, advice is always helpful, but advice should never be dominating the trades that you're making. At the end of the day, you are the one in the driver's seat. It is ultimately your responsibility.

What: This section of your post-trading analysis should include factors such as the purchase price, the stop-loss price (if there is one), the profit and loss analysis, the strategy that you used, and the industry group that you used. This is much more straightforward than the "who" section. A good idea that many investors use for this section of their post-trading analysis is to create a template that they can fill in as they go. This usually cuts down on the time that they spend on the post-trading analysis.

When: this section might also benefit from a template. You should include factors such as the date that you made the trade and the date in which you saw profits in this section. Of course, this is day trading, so the date purchased and the date sold are likely going to be the same; however, in my other book we already briefly discussed how day trading does not always mean that the share is bought and sold in the same day. Sometimes, day traders are so specific about this section of their post-trading analysis that they know the exact hour and minute in which they became profitable. You don't have to start out being this specific, but you may eventually find that this type of information is useful in the long-term.

Where: Where were you when you were making this trade? Were you at your home office, or were you trading on your mobile device that day? Of course, this section might not be as important as other sections of the post-trading analysis, but you might end up finding it to be extremely important depending on your overall lifestyle. For example, if you have kids and are trying to balance between taking care of them and day trading, you might find that when you're distracted while trading on your mobile device, your decision-making skills are compromised. While many investors often find this section to be a bit useless at times, that's not to say that you shouldn't take it seriously.

Why: Lastly, you should be thinking about why you even made the trade from the jump. This section should have many details in it, so that you can have an idea of your thought process during the initial time of purchase. It might even be useful to think of this section as journal-like in quality. If you think of it, document the emotions that you were feeling at the time as well. The best traders are those who don't have emotions while they trade, but it will likely take years to get to this point. For example, if you sold too early because of fear associated with the trade, then you know that you have improvements to make.

Day Trading Mistake 7: You Describe Your Deals and Trades with Emotional Words

This might seem silly, but one of the mistakes that many day traders in particular make is that they use emotional words to describe how their day is going on the stock market. These words include ones such as "hope", "wish", and "feel". If you find that you say or even think in this manner, then you know that you have some emotional work to do in regards to day trading. Another indicator that can suggest that you are too emotional in your trades is if you find that you often call loved ones as you make money on your trades. This type of behavior indicates that you're too personally invested in your stocks. Without your conscious knowledge, your emotions could be the reason why you are making trades, and this is a huge mistake that even seasoned day trading investors make. While some day traders might be successful with this type of strategy in the short term, in the long term it ends up ruining any investment credibility that they had.

Day Trading Mistake 8: Ignoring Correlations

A correlation can be best defined as when one factor influences another. Positive correlation is when both variables are moving in the same direction, while negative correlation is when both variables are moving in the opposite direction.

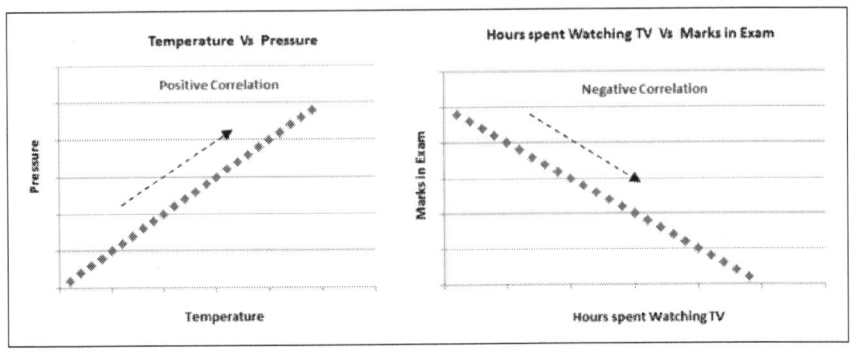

As you can see from the table above, on the left we have a positive correlation and on the right, we have a negative correlation. On the left, the more pressure there is, the higher the temperature is going to be. These variables are moving in the same direction. Contrastingly, on the right, the more hours that are spent watching television, the lower the marks on the exam are going to be. In this example, the variables are moving in the opposite direction. The stock market also includes correlations, and if you ignore these factors then it can increase your overall risk. Many investors think that if they trade on different markets that it will decrease their overall risk, but this is actually the opposite of the truth. All of the markets are correlated with one another, so it doesn't matter if you invest in multiple markets. Your risk will remain the same or even increase if you don't know what you're doing. Cross-market correlations are always going to increase your risk, and if you decide to invest in multiple markets without noticing correlations between markets (both positive and negative correlations), then you could potentially be setting yourself up for failure.

Day Trading Mistake 9: You Have a Formulated Percentage that

You Always Risk

If you've already read my book on advanced stock trading secrets, then you are already aware of the fact that putting down less than ten percent during a stop-loss is usually pretty fruitless because after commission costs you're not going to see much in terms of profit. Besides a stop-loss order though, you really should be taking each trade in stride and considering each percentage that you're risking in stride.

Day Trading Mistake 10: You Don't Strive to Minimize Your Costs

Especially for day traders, commission costs and other types of fees are prone to sneak up on you. The reality is that a day trader is often trading multiple stocks throughout the day and these shares almost always have fees attached to them. Unless you can convince your broker to cut a deal with you where you are only paying an annual fee for using their services, it would definitely behoove you to figure out how you can cut transaction costs in any way that you can. The first step to doing this, if you're not already, is to keep close track of what kind of money you're losing on every transaction that you make. If you can figure out on average how much money you're losing, you can work to close the gap between your profits and your losses.

Chapter 2:

The Notion and Strategy of Contrarian Trading

Now that you know some of the mistakes that advanced traders just like you are perhaps making without being fully aware of it, this next chapter is going to focus on one type of advanced strategy that you can use to take your day trading endeavors to the next level. Contrarian trading, while it can be risky, can also be pretty profitable when used correctly and within the right market climate. Once you know what contrarian trading is, you'll be able to implement this trading strategy in conjunction with supplemental tips that will be provided in a subsequent chapter. Let's take a look at what contrarian trading is, how you can use it, an the advantages and disadvantages that exist within this type of trading.

What is Contrarian Trading?

Contrarian trading can best be defined as an investment strategy type that counters how the market is doing during a certain period of time. For example, investors who use contrarian trading often pick up stocks when the market is not doing well, and they choose to sell when the market is doing well again. A contrarian investor buys and sells shares in this manner with the overall belief that the market is doing "well" from the public's perspective when most investors have already invested to their personal maximum capacity. On the other hand, when the market is doing "poorly" from the public's perspective, this means that most of the players on the stock market have already sold out of their stocks and now have the capital to purchase more. From this perspective, the market can only go up from here because people are looking to get more money into new investments quickly. This is where the contrarian investor can thrive. Basically, contrarian investors deliberately go against what the popular sentiment is.

For example, let's say that Apple as a company is struggling with their popularity and usefulness of their products ever since the passing of Steve Jobs (this isn't so far from the truth, now is it?) In a way, it can be perceived that Apple is being unfairly targeted as a company that is less well off now that their founder has passed, and so their overall stock goes down for the time being. If a contrarian investor noticed that the purchasing price of Apple's stock decreased immediately after Steve Job's died, he or she might get excited because this can be perceived as a drop in share price for an arbitrary reason. We all know now that Steve Job's passing did not ultimately result in the collapse of Apple, and that the company as a whole is continuing to produce products that are both useful to the public and innovative in their technological capacity. Believing in contrarian theory, a contrarian investor would start buying stocks of Apple at the lower price as soon as the rest of the investors started to get rid of their shares. They are banking and trusting the fact that the popular decision to get rid of Apple shares will only be temporary in nature, and that after the news of Steve Job's death has passed, investors will once again begin to invest in shares of Apple at a similar top-dollar price. This is the essence of contrarian investing. Hopefully this example has made the concept a bit clearer for you.

It's Not As Simple as You May Think

Of course, the example above was an idealized version of contrarian theory in the hopes that the clearest concept of it could be conveyed to you. While it can be seen in the example above that the contrarian investor would take the opposite stance on their investment upon hearing of Steve Job's death, this certainly does not mean that the contrarian investor would immediately despise a stock that's doing well. Instead of simply looking for stocks that are doing well and waiting for them to collapse, the contrarian investor looks for evidence that the established trends of the stock are doing well despite the public sentiment at the time. This is why the example about Steve Jobs is a good one. While it can be slightly predictable that the stock of Apple would decrease in value after the death of Steve Jobs, the reality is that the company was not staying afloat through his doings alone. Obviously, Apple is a conglomerate of many people at this point in time. Jobs' death was one event that changed the public opinion of Apple's ability to conduct business for only a short period of time, instead of changing for the long-term. The reality is that at some point, the people who once got out of Apple are going to realize that the stock is still viable, and this is when the contrarian investor profits. He or she has already purchased the stock when it was "down and out" and now is profiting from investors who are reentering the market.

Markers for Which the Contrarian Investor Should Look

Now that you know the basics of being a contrarian investor, the next step is to be able to think like one from a stock market and day trading perspective. Below is a list of indicators that can help you to figure out when to buy and sell stock with the contrarian mentality in mind. When going over this section, it's important to keep in mind that contrarian investors are preying upon the market sentiment as a whole. As a contrarian, your job is not merely to notice the sentiments of the market; you have to be able to quantify them in a way that makes logical and numerical sense. These tips should inform you on how to do just that:

Contrarian Trading Tip 1: Purchase your Stocks through Put Options

In case you have never heard of it before, a put option is a stock that is traded on or before a specified date in time. The logic behind purchasing a put option is that an investor is selling a share on or before a specific date because he or she thinks that the market for this particular stock is going to fall in price around that date. If you are looking for put options, you should be looking for many of them occurring within one specific stock. If you can find a trend of put options, then you know that the popular sentiment within this stock is that it's going to decrease on or before a pre-defined date in time. When you purchase a put option, the idea is that you can ride the wave of profits that are going to exist as the price of the stock increases through the selling of these put options. It's important to recognize the moment when you should sell this type of stock, and you will have to look at the climate and unique situation of the stock in order to figure this out. For example, if there is talk on the news that this stock's company is going to be releasing a controversial technology within the next few weeks, this would be a reason why you might decide to hold onto the stock or to sell it. You would have to respond to this activity in a way that makes sense to you in that specific situation.

Contrarian Trading Tip 2: Take Analytical Ratings into Consideration

Everyone has most likely seen news segments about the stock market. These types of shows often offer free advice on how investors should be trading their stocks, and if you watch these shows they can provide you with an indication of how people are responding to the stock in general. For example, if you are watching one of these shows and see that the announcer or newsperson is not suggesting that people should be buying a particular stock even though it's increasing in value, this might be a reason why a contrarian would decide to purchase it. It's obvious to see why a contrarian would value this type of stock; while everyone else is not being told to purchase it, the contrarian is eager to invest in a stock that nonetheless looks valuable despite the popular sentiment. Whether you want to believe it or not, television analysts do influence the way in which people make trades, and as a contrarian investor you would certainly be able to prey upon this fact.

Contrarian Trading Tip 3: Purchasing Short Sells

The last contrarian tip that this book can offer to you is to purchase short stocks. In case you're currently unfamiliar, a short sell is a stock that is not actually owned by the investor. Instead, the share of the stock that is purchase is owned by a third party entirely. What this basically means is that if anything that happens to the stock while you're in possession of it, this is your financial responsibility. On the other hand, you do not actually own the stock and this means that if the brokerage firm who lent it to you needs it back for any reason, they can take it back from you without any explanation. For obvious reasons, short selling a stock can be risky for any investor, and the transaction costs for this type of investment are also usually particularly high because you typically have to pay the broker as well as the person who actually owns the stock. Anyway, from a contrarian's point of view, purchasing a short sell can be beneficial in the same way that purchasing a put option can be.

Additionally, purchasing a short sell is often perfect for a day trader because it's definitely ill-advised to hold onto a short sell for a long period of time. One of the biggest reasons why any type of investor should work against purchasing a short sell and hold onto it for a while is because these types of shares are not charged interest directly to the money that's earned against it. Instead, a broker usually charges this interest to the investor's account that they have with the broker as a whole, and this type of interest usually accrues more quickly than it does when it's tied directly to the money itself.

Lastly, one of the surest ways to figure out whether there is positive or negative sentiment behind a short sell is to look at the interest that's being accrued on it when the investor is trying to sell it. For example, if you see that there is a fair amount of interest tied to the stock, you can infer that the person is trying to sell the stock based on the notion that the stock is going to drop in price soon. Just as you were advised to do with the put option, it's also recommended that you look for many shares that are being sold as short within a specific company's stock. This is yet another way to recognize when the overall sentiment for this particular company is negative rather than positive.

The Advantages of Contrarian Trading

The biggest advantage that any contrarian investor is banking on is the fact that many investors play the market through their emotions rather than through logic. From the contrarian perspective, this is an additional reason why they are prone to looking for those investors who are making short-term decisions through short sales and put options, rather than those who are in it for the long haul. If you are thinking about using the contrarian theory as a staple in your investment strategy, know that the general investor emotional chart ranges on one end from fear and swings to greed on the opposite end of the spectrum. A chart has been included below to bring this concept to life for you.

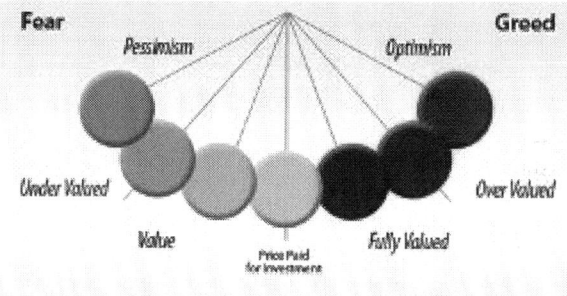

Many, many investors have made a fortune by resisting the urge to partake in mass hysteria and fear during times of distress in the market. This type of emotional investing has been going on since the beginning of the stock market in the eighteen-hundreds. We all know that if anything remains consistent from century-to-century, it's human emotions. Human emotions are what keep the subject of book trends like Romeo and Juliet popular to the present day. While the market can change from one day to the next, you have the consistency of human emotions to keep you grounded within the contrarian theory.

The Risks of Contrarian Trading

The biggest risk that exists for contrarian trading is when you decide that you're going to use the contrarian investment strategy and there is little to no evidence that there is an actual sentimental trend occurring within the market. Remember, the basis of contrarian trading is all about how you are able to identify and quantify emotional trends. If you don't see any trends that indicate this, it's likely that you're going to be dealing with unemotional investors who are going to take your money and your shirt along with it. When you do see a trend, it's likely that you're going to be dealing with investors who are relatively new to the market. When you don't see a trend, there's a chance that you'll find yourself in a situation where you're dealing with people who are going to swindle you out of the capital in which you seek.

A Final Word on the Contrarian Strategy

Now that you know all about what contrarian investing is, how is works and the pros and cons associated with this mentality, the last piece of advice that I will leave you with is about ways that you can track sentimental trends in the market. Of course, skilled contrarian investors do not simply use their wit in order to figure out the trending sentiments of the day. Some sources that experienced contrarian theorists use include the following:

Sentiment Surveys: Surveys from sources such as the American Association of Individual Investors can help you to figure out the general sentiment in the stock market.

These types of surveys are usually published weekly, so they are perfect for the day trader.

The Volatility Index: The volatility index, also known as simply the "VIX" seeks to calculate the general fear that exists in the market. It doesn't stop there. After it has calculated the fear that has encouraged investors to buy and sell their stock, it then estimates that total volatility on the S&P 500 for the next thirty days.

The Put-Call Ratio: The put-call ratio measures the bearish-to-bullish shares that were traded over a certain period of time in order to figure out the mood of the market in its entirety. Noticing bear and bullish trends in the market should already be something that is fairly common to you at this point, and if it's not then you should head back to my first book on the beginner's guide to day trading and go over the chapter on candlestick charts again.

Chapter 3:

How Momentum Trading Works

If you're not much for recognizing sentimental activity amongst investors and you'd rather stick to something more logical, then the next strategy about which we're going to discuss is known as momentum trading. After you're finished reading this chapter, you should be able to discern which day trading strategy you'd like to employ more. Of course, it is possible to have multiple day trading strategies at your disposal, so that you can use different strategies in different situations. How are you supposed to know which strategy to use if you don't know about different types? Let's get started talking about how momentum trading works and the advantages that exist for you when you employ it.

What is Momentum Trading?

Momentum trading is when investors pinpoint stocks that are moving in one direction at a high volume. This means that not only are these stocks swinging wildly from one side to another, but this activity is being seen from multiple investors at the same time. Depending on the climate of the market, the momentum trader might hold their position within the market for an entire day, for only a couple of hours, or merely for a few short minutes. As you can see from the lengths of time that were just given, this strategy is one that is popular amongst day traders. This strategy can be seen as being the opposite of the type of trading strategy that was discussed in the previous chapter because momentum traders actually try to "ride along" with the popular stocks of the day instead of try to bet against them. While the momentum philosophy to trading can be seen as being at odds with contrarian investors, they can also be seen as similar. You see, similar to contrarian traders, a momentum trader will use certain indicators to prey upon sentiments that are popular throughout the day, but he or she will be using sentiment as a primary indicator for movement. Let's take a look at some of the indicators that might influence a momentum trader:

Momentum Trading Indicator 1: Message Boards

Often times, a momentum-based trader will be up before the crows, researching message boards and other types of online forums that will help to give away which stocks will have the greatest amount of volatility throughout the day. For a momentum-interested investor, volatility is measured in the following ways:

Volatility is a statistical measurement: Volatility, when used for momentum trading, is measured primarily through statistics. It is basically measured by using the techniques of standard deviation. Standard deviation is when you take the mean (or average) of statistical data and look at the actual dispersion of the data from this mean result. In financial settings, standard deviation is typically applied through the analysis of the rate of return of an investment, and this rate of return is then used to figure out the volatility and the stock's volatile history. The general rule on the subject is that the higher the standard deviation is, the more volatile the market. From this type of statistical finding, it's obvious to see already that momentum trading is much for math-centered than is contrarian investing. Once you understand how to calculate the standard deviation, you are able to calculate how volatile a particular stock is within the larger market. In general, the standard deviation can be calculated using three variables. These variables are:

- The mean value

- The variance value

- The square root value

As a quick refresher, the mean value of something can be determined by adding all of the values of something together and then dividing it by the total number of factors that were originally added. For example, if we have three numbers such as 8, 5, and 2, we would add all of these numbers up to find a total of 15. We would then divide this number 15 by the total numbers that were originally added together, which in this case is three. This means that the mean for these three numbers, or the average for these three numbers collectively is 5.

The variance is determined by subtracting this mean value from the data points of the equation. In this situation and for our purposes, the data points would be the rates of return that we see in the market as a whole. The rate of return is also known as the return on investment, and can be calculated using the following formula:

Return on Investment = (Gain from Investment − Cost of Investment) / Cost of Investment

Using the formula that was given above, it should be fairly easy for you to pinpoint your data points based on the investments that are in your portfolio and the ones that you are seeing on the market during a particular period of time. After you have both your data points based on the equation from the ROI and your mean, you can subtract the mean from each data point. After you've gotten this subtracted number, you then square it for each individual answer that you've obtained, and then add all of these squared numbers together.

Finally, in order to obtain the standard deviation for which you're looking, you would simply take the square root of the number that you just calculated. This would provide you with the standard deviation that you need for a particular share of stock. If you were looking for the volatility of a particular stock, you would then have to compare these standard deviated numbers from one another in order to figure out how volatile the market is. This is the work that momentum traders typically put into their work before the market even opens. Talk about being busy!

Momentum Trading Indicator 2: The News

Surfing the message boards in the morning will certainly help the momentum trader figure out which stocks are the "hot" stocks for the day; however, the daily news will also help them to figure this out too. As the momentum trader searches for volatility, he or she always has his or her ears open for news and press releases about stock-related companies. This too can be helpful in determining which stocks are going to see large amounts of movement throughout the day.

These are two of the most common ways in which a momentum trader will begin their day. He or she will most basically be looking for the "momentum" that exists in the market, and this is the type of activity that will dominate their activity for the remainder of the day. Once the stock market has actually opened and the momentum trader has finished his or her preliminary research, their next step is to look at the list of initial stocks that are being traded at long in comparison to the list that he or she has compiled during his preliminary research period earlier in the day. Some of the factors for which he or she is looking include answering some of the following questions:

- Are the stocks that he or she has chosen during the preliminary market assessment rising in price or lowering in price?

- Are these stocks not only increasing in price, but are they increasing in an astronomical way?

- Are these stocks generally acting in a way that is consistent with the preliminary research that was done in the morning before the market opened?

As should be obvious through these types of questions, the preliminary research that a day trader with a momentum focus does is arguably more important than the actual trading that he or she will be doing throughout the rest of the day. If their research is off during their preliminary research period, then it's clear to see that they will be pretty much at a disadvantage for the rest of the day while they're trading. This is why the preliminary research phase is extremely important for momentum traders. If he or she can't figure out which stocks are going to be moving the most throughout the day, then he or she will be at a loss until the stock market closes once more.

After the top stocks for the day have been compiled by the New York Stock Exchange or a different trading entity (basically whichever entity that you're using to trade), the momentum investor will then narrow his or her list down significantly and will only choose to focus his or her attention on the strongest stocks of the day. The "strongest" stocks in the eyes of a momentum trader are those stocks that look like they're increasing in value more quickly than the other stocks on the market. The hope that the momentum-focused investor has at this point is that their list somewhat matches the list that they ultimately compile once the stock market actually opens.

The Notion of the Momentum Indicator:

So far, we have looked at how the momentum trader uses their time in the wee hours of the morning in order to maximize the potential for profit later in the day. After the momentum trader has finalized the list of stocks on which they're going to focus their attention for the rest of the day, they will then turn their attention to analyzing one of the primary indicators for their specific niche. This tool is known as the momentum indicator. A chart illustrating the momentum indicator has been provided for your convenience below.

The momentum indicator is a tool that looks at the net changes of a stock over the course of a day and over the course of some predefined time stamps. Obviously, the day trader wants to obtain data that focuses on the history of a stock over the course of a day, rather than look at the history of a stock from the perspective of days at a time. As you can see from the chart above, the momentum line is plotted along the same line as the "price" indicator. This makes it easy to see the momentum of the stock from a financial perspective. As you can see, when the momentum line traces upward, this means that the market is more volatile than when it is moving to a downward position.

It's important to note here that a momentum-focused trader will often use a tool that was introduced in my beginner's guide in order to see how the stock is doing throughout the day. Yes, this means that we are circling back around to the subject of the Level II Quotes tool with which you may already be familiar. Once the investor has their momentum indicator up and running, he or she will use the Level II Quotes to watch for when bids start to appear and line up for the stocks that are moving the fastest in the market for that particular day. This is where the concept of a "breakout" becomes important. A breakout can be best defined as a price movement that is predefined by a certain level of resistance. If the investor has their Level II Quotes page up and running prior to the breakout, the orders that they see lining up behind a certain stock will show them when the breakout is more likely to occur. Breakouts are typically defined by high volumes of stocks being traded, and this also increases volatility. If a momentum trader is good at what he or she does, then it means that this investor will have already anticipated this volatility through their analysis of the numbers that they calculated through standard deviation.

Once the breakout period has been identified, the momentum trader is not usually concerned about being one of the first or second traders in the market. He or she is basically looking to only purchase their stock at the market price, rather than get in a price lower than what other people are paying. What's more important than the point in which the momentum trader purchases stock is the moment at which he or she exits the deal. Once the momentum trader picks up the stock, his or her anxiety truly begins. This type of investor watches both the momentum chart and the Level II Quote and tries to figure out whether or not the up-trend is going to continue over a long period of time or if it is only going to last for a few short minutes. As was previously stated, this up tick is what determines whether the momentum trader keeps his or her stock for a day, an hour, or a minute. As should be obvious to you by this point, momentum trading can prove to cause large levels of stress depending on the day.

The Advantages of Momentum Trading

The biggest advantage that exists for a day trader is that it is possible to earn a lot of money in only a short period of time when the day trader calculates the breakout period correctly. If a momentum-focused trader can get good at what he or she does, the possibility exists for he or she to walk away from the day having made big profits. Of course, even if you are a good and skilled momentum trader, you're going to lose money sometimes. This is a fact that is not exclusive to momentum traders, but to the market as a whole. You need to live with the fact that everyday cannot be a winning one on the stock market. For a day trader, this fact is usually realized more quickly than with other types of trading through which you can partake.

The Disadvantages to Momentum Trading

One of the first disadvantages that a new momentum trader can see is that the probationary period for this type of investment strategy is typically longer than other types that exist. It's likely that it's going to take you a while to simply get the first part of this strategy right. Waking up early and practicing how to target the most volatile stocks for the day is the best way to figure out how you can be a successful practitioner of momentum trading, and for this reason many prospering momentum traders quit after only a week or two. It's common for people to become frustrated quickly because it's often hard to predict the top stocks for the day.

Another disadvantage that is an unfortunate reality of day trading involves the time that it takes out of your day. Unlike other types of trading strategies, the momentum-focused trading strategy is one that simply takes all day to implement correctly. Of course, if you can figure out the ins and outs of it and are seeing profits more than you're seeing losses, the time that it takes won't really matter to you; however, because of the trial-and error that it usually takes to get this strategy right, it's likely that you're not going to be seeing great gains in the beginning. If you have a lot of time to burn and you're hell-bent on learning this strategy properly, then more power to you; however, the reality is that these days time is always of the essence. If time is a concern to you and you are looking to jump start your momentum trading endeavors, a great way to supplement this is to hire a mentor or find someone who is already using the momentum trading strategy often. A great idea would even be to get to a point where you are making decisions on your own in real time with a seasoned investor by your side, helping you to make the right decisions along the way. This type of experience will likely get you to a point of success faster than if you were to go it alone.

Chapter 4:

How to Keep a Day Trading Journal and Why It's Important

As was already stated before we started our discussion on specific advanced day trading strategies, it might be necessary for you to go back and reevaluate the key points of each one before you actually start to use it in a real-time setting. Now that you have a basic understanding of two advanced strategies that many day traders use on a regular basis, we are going to turn attention away from the technicalities of strategies and towards the idea of recordkeeping. One of the things that many experienced day traders tout is the importance of keeping some sort of trade journal. This chapter will focus on what to include in a trade journal and why it's important. As you will see in a few moments, the trade journal is often similar to the post-trading analysis that we've already discussed, but it also differs in terms of detail. Let's take a look at what you should be including in your trade journal, and then we will focus on why it's important to create one and upkeep it.

What Should You Be Including in Your Trade Journal?

1. Did Your Trade Work as You Expected It To?

One of first aspects that you need to consider as you look to write entries into your trade journal is whether or not the trade worked out in the same way that you originally thought it would. Often times when trading on the stock market, things have a tendency to not go as planned. If you find that this is the case when you're making deals for yourself, then you need to address the areas that strayed from what you had in your head before the trading began. While you're documenting this information, it's important to keep in mind that often times the strategy behind your trade can differ from what actually happens when there's money as stake. Again, this could be for a variety of reasons, including the fact that emotions could be influencing the trades that you're making. Be open to being honest with yourself about whether or not a trade went right or wrong. This will help you to see not only your areas of weakness but also your areas of strength and this will help you in your overall long term stock strategies

2. What is Your Stop Limit and Why Did You Set It There?

Once you've documented whether or not your trade strategy work out as you intended it to, the next concept that you should be documenting is your stop limit. Your stop limit is the amount of money that you're willing to lose in a trade. Often times, even seasoned investors in the heat of the moment will stray from their stop limit because they are eager to make money where it doesn't exist. Documenting what your stop limit is, the reason why you set it there, and whether or not you stuck to your stop limit can help you to figure out how disciplined you are in sticking to your stock market strategy over the course of the day and whether or not you need to check yourself as the day progresses. Another reason why documenting this type of information is important is because it will most likely ultimately lead you to realizing that you need to have a firm grasp on how much money you're going to be spending throughout the day on each investment. Again, this aspect of the trading journey is mostly there to reinforce the idea of discipline into your trading strategy.

3. What Did You Choose to Trade and Why?

Lastly, one of the key elements that is included into any successful and serious investor's trade journal is documentation of which stocks they traded throughout the day and why. So many investors back up their investment strategies with reasons that include that the price of a particular stock has risen or fallen to the amount that is "just right", without backing it up with any substantial information. This isn't a good type of strategy, and writing down your reasoning for purchasing a particular stock will help you to see whether or not your stock choices are grounded in substantial logic. What's even worse is that sometimes traders will choose to purchase and sell stock out of merely a feeling of boredom. This too can end up having disastrous consequences. It's likely that a trader may not be aware of the fact that he or she is trading out of boredom or because the market is moving "just right" for them, and often times having a trade journal will force these people to be awakened to these types of facts. This is yet another reason why a trade journal can be beneficial.

Why is a Trade Journal Important?

Now that you know that you should be including in your trade journal, this next section of the chapter is going to look at why trade journals are important. Hopefully after reading this section, you will be able to see why you need to start using one. One of the great things about the prevalence of computers is that you can easily create templates for yourself and quickly insert this information at the end of each trading day. Even if you are not that thrilled about documenting your experience as a day trader at the end of each trading day, you should still be willing to do it at least once a week. Now that you have hopefully come to understand the type of information the is generally found in a trade journal, let's take a look at some of the reasons why a trade journal can be beneficial to you.

Reason 1 Why You Need a Trade Journal: Review

Some of the best day traders go over their trade journal in the morning before they start their trades for the rest of the day. By doing this, they are clearing and focusing their mind on the mistakes and good things that they did the day before. Another good tactic that the top traders typically implement is that they will write down key notes that they learned at the end of the day for that particular day. Over time, you will be able to simply look at the key information from each day, and this will eliminate the need to sift through entire pages of information when you've for what you're looking. Over time and day-by-day, you will be growing and educating yourself as an investor, and this activity only takes a few moments each morning.

Reason 2 Why You Need a Trade Journal: Improvement

The second reason why you really should be considering keeping a trading journal if you're not already is because it gives you the ability to improve upon areas of yourself and your trading patterns. For example, successful investors will usually take the time to look at the points when they entered and exited a trade in order to figure out whether or not they could have improved these points with the information they had at that particular moment in time. This is the type of contemplation that often separates the winners from the losers, and a day trading journal is where it at all starts.

Reason 3 Why You Need a Trade Journal: Emotional Check

The last reason why you should consider keeping a day trading journal is so that you can keep your emotions in check. Emotional trading is often one of the aspects of trading that many investors forget about, but it can also be the silent killer that causes deals to go south. It might even be beneficial for you to document each day the emotions that were surrounding particular decisions, so that you can focus some of your energy on eliminating these feelings over time.

Chapter 5:

Ways to Manage Your Time as a Day Trader

This book has been chalk-full of techniques and strategies that you can use to grow your existing or aspiring day trading strategies, but we have yet to talk about day trading in a sense that goes beyond the strategies within day trading. Of course, everyone who participates in day trading has a life and it is extremely important that this life is not compromised because of the desire to win money. We have all heard horror stories of people who become obsessed with the stock market and end up throwing their children's tuition down the toilet. Don't let this happen to you! This chapter will focus on how you can best manage your time as a day trader, so that you don't have to choose between a life of happiness and a life that is dominated by stock market greed.

Time Management Technique 1: Choose a Trading Strategy that Meshes with Your Personality and Lifestyle

One of the most important factors for any day trader is to choose a strategy that coincides rather than contrasts that individual's overall personality and character. For example, if you're the type of person who can be patient amidst chaos and you are able to naturally resist the urge to sell and purchase stock through fear or anxiety, then the truth of the matter is that the lifestyle of a traditional stock trader might work better for you than would the life of a day trader. If on the other hand, you find that you are constantly antsy and can't stop thinking about what you're going to do with your money next, then the life of a day trader is right up your ally. This example is certainly not to try and convince you that day trading isn't for you, but if you are somewhat laidback, then don't you think that day trading is going to cause you anxiety that you're not traditionally used to experiencing? Your trading strategy should coincide with your overall personality, and this requires that you know yourself well enough to choose a trading method that works well for you.

Time Management Technique 2: Take the Time to Look at Charts

Of course, there are areas of day trading that you might be able to skim over and still be successful, but ignoring charts and empirical information is not one of these factors. Even if you don't have much time on your hands, looking at and understanding a chart prior to investing in a stock is far more important than performing guesswork and hoping for the best. If there's anything that you should take from this book it's this: take the time to understand empirical data, and if you don't have the time then don't bother wasting your money on a trade.

Time Management Technique 3: Learn to Systematically Absorb Information

We have already discussed the fact that you can develop templates for yourself for when you're writing in your trade journal and conducting a post-trading analysis. Time management should be no different. Success often comes from the little things, the detailed information that is sought after and calculated day in and day out. Having a systematic and disciplined way of processing information will keep you working towards the same thing every day, and this creates predictability. Often, it's much easier to be successful when you have a process that works for you, rather than finding that you're all over the map.

Time Management Technique 4: Don't Try to Force Time

When I say, "Don't try to force time", what I really mean is that you should never try to force a deal if the conditions that you'd like to see simply aren't there. If you're always eager to trade constantly and quickly, you are going to make mistakes and these mistakes are ones that often could have been avoided if you had been more patient. To reiterate, many day traders are in disbelief when they hear that other successful day traders sometimes go days without making a trade, but this is the truth of the matter. You don't have to force trades if they just aren't there for you, and you don't have to make a trade every single day just because you're a "day" trader. If you're uncomfortable with the conditions of a certain trade, listen to your instincts. Even if it turns out that you're ultimately wrong and you find out that you should have traded after all, you'll at least be privy to this knowledge without having invested any money in it in order to find out.

Time Management Technique 5: Avoid Distractions

Of course, most investors want to be watching the news in the morning so that they can get a feeling for the climate of the market on a particular day, but often times the news eventually starts recycling itself and the television becomes more background noise than anything that's concretely useful. This type of background noise can quickly go from being helpful information to being an unnecessary distraction. It's important that you can delineate between the two. A good plan for yourself would be to set a time for when the television is on and when it's time to turn it off. Additionally, you can do the same thing for your phone. Have your phone on during certain hours of the day, and turn it off turn peak trading hours. This again requires discipline. Lastly, avoid the temptation to go down the rabbit-hole of watching YouTube videos or surfing Facebook. These tasks that you think will only take a minute end up taking entire hours of your time, and before you know it you're losing tons of money.

Time management may not seem like a necessary topic to cover when discussing the stock market, but for a day trader time management is often essential to overall success. This is particularly true when discussing the strategies of both the contrarian and momentum philosophy. If you have a family, time management and the stock market is essential. Even if you think that you could earn money during all times of the day, having a balance between when you should be trading and when you should be spending time with your loved ones if often essential to maintaining your sanity.

Conclusion

Thank for making it through to the end of *Day Trading: The Advanced Guide that Will Make You the KING of Day Traders*, let's hope it was informative and able to provide you with all of the tools you need to achieve your goals whatever it may be. The strategies of both the contrarian philosophy and the momentum-philosophy are sure to take your day trading strategies to the next level. It's important to remember that these strategies can be used interchangeably; however, it is generally advised that you master one technique before advancing to learning the other technique. Don't get frustrated if these techniques don't come to you naturally. They will often take a lot of time and you'll have to work out the kinks of each one before implementing them in real time. Persevere through these tougher times and you're sure to find success.

The next step is to go back and look at the strategies that you already have in place. It's likely that there is at least one area of your overall trading strategy that can be tweaked your altered based on the copious amounts of information that were presented in this book.

Finally, if you found this book useful in anyway, a review on Amazon is always appreciated!

Made in the USA
Middletown, DE
02 April 2018